THE COMPLETE FLAT COATED RETRIEVER

The author with Rase Lysander Flat Coat Retriever and Ch Dagill Solitair of Rase BMD.

THE COMPLETE
FLAT COATED RETRIEVER

Paddy Petch

The Boydell Press . Howell Book House

First published 1988 by The Boydell Press
an imprint of Boydell & Brewer Ltd
PO Box 9, Woodbridge, Suffolk IP12 3DF
and by Howell Book House Inc.
230 Park Avenue, New York, N.Y.10169, USA

ISBN 0 85115 463 8

British Library Cataloguing in Publication Data

Petch, Paddy
    The complete flat-coated retriever.
    1. Flat-coated retriever
    I. Title
    636.7'52   SF429.F45
    ISBN 0–85115–463–8

Library of Congress Cataloging in Publication Data applied for

Printed in Great Britain by
St Edmundsbury Press Ltd, Bury St Edmunds, Suffolk

CONTENTS

INTRODUCTION

Since I wrote my first book on the Flat Coated Retriever in 1980 the breed numbers have increased so quickly that now entries at a Championship Show are very seldom below the hundred mark, despite the high cost of the classes. My original book obviously fulfilled the need for which it was written, and now that it is unobtainable I thought the time had come to produce another guide to this doyen of the gundog breeds.

This book, like the last, has been written particularly with the newcomer in mind, but will be of interest to all devotees of this character dog with the boundless enthusiasm and endlessly wagging tail. Recognised by the Kennel Club in the 1880s the Flat Coat is one of life's optimists, the epitome of the canine extrovert. He is always ready for a game, a walk, or a drive in the car. Friendly to the extreme, he is nevertheless a very good guard and his deep bark loudly warns of people about. Often called the original 'laughing dog' the Flat Coat has a wicked sense of humour, coupled with an inborn love of water, a natural retrieving aptitude and a dependence on human company that makes this dog a joy to all who own one of nature's gentlemen.

Paddy Petch

1

Origins of the Breed

The oldest of the retriever breeds is the Labrador, which is followed by the Curly Coat with the Flat Coat in third place. Like so many of the early dogs, the origins of the breed are lost in the mists of time but almost certainly the 'Wavy Coat', as the predecessors of our modern dogs were called, were among the most complex in makeup, the result of the intermingling of many breeds thus giving much mixed blood in the final product. Early retriever records are very inaccurate, for apparently any type of dog who would fetch back game was loosely designated as a retriever whether of the bulldog, terrier or mongrel types. As long as they would retrieve from land or water they were much in demand as guns and shooting became a rich man's sport. In the fullness of time the qualities of the land spaniels and water dogs were recognised as particularly suited to the job, and by dint of selective breeding, sportsmen developed these breeds individually, rather as branches grow out from the trunk of a tree.

There eventually emerged two definite breeds, spaniels and setters. These were produced by cross-breeding, incorporating collies and sheepdogs (introduced for their intelligent working). The setters, it is thought, were the descendants of land spaniels crossed with pointers. In Nancy Laughton's book *Review of the Flat Coated Retriever* there is mention of black Irish Setters seen by Richardson as quoted by Edward Ash in his book *Dogs: Their History and Development*. Dr Laughton also mentions Edward Laverack's book written in 1872 which describes a strain of black setters found in Wales. Some notables of the day – the Earl of Tankerville, Lord Home and Mr Harry Rothwell – also kept these Welsh black Setters. In 1914 Charles Eley, author of the *History of Retrievers*, was of the opinion that everything pointed to the retrieving setter being the forerunner of the Wavy Coated Retriever, as the breed first became known around 1850. He suggested that it was very likely that the Irish/Welsh black Setters were the dogs in question, with some blood from the big black and tan Gordon Setters. These originated from Scotland, where they were commonly used for retrieving from the 1860s onwards. It was the necessity to improve the power of these dogs in water, Eley suggests, that led to cross breeding them with a

The old type of Flat Coat.
(*Hutchinson's* Dog Encyclopaedia, *photograph: E. C. Reid*)

small dog from Newfoundland known as the St John's Dog which was first brought to Britain by the lumber ships of the early 1800s. The Labrador also comes from this strain, and Colonel Peter Hawker reported having seen the latter in Newfoundland as early as 1814.

As a result of crossing the Collie, the Setter (black and/or Gordon) and the St John's Dog, a heavy, wavy coated dog, looking not unlike a smaller, slimmer edition of the present day Newfoundland, was produced. Eley records that these dogs had 'a broad shortish skull very heavily stocked; an animal big in bone frequently showing a rolling gait due to weak quarters'. The tan and brindle colours inherited from their ancestors was often shown in these early dogs but it was laid down within a fairly short time that black for the Flat Coated Retriever should be the acceptable colour. The person responsible for this fixing of colour and type was Dr Bond Moore of Wolverhampton.

But the acknowledged 'father' of the Flat Coat breed was Mr Sewallis Evelyn Shirley (1844–1904) of Ettington Park, Stratford on Avon (at one time the Conservative Member of Parliament for County Monaghan). Mr Shirley also has a claim to fame in that he founded the Kennel Club in 1873, holding office as its first President and Chairman of Committee. He was attracted by this new breed and sought to stabilise the breeding. Fortunately being wealthy he could proceed to do this regardless of time or money. He purchased some of the puppies of Old Bounce and her daughter Young Bounce who were bred by the Redditch gamekeeper Mr D. Hull. According to Charles Eley again, these animals were the original strain from which all present day Flat Coats are descended. Mr Shirley also purchased stock from Dr Bond Moore and Mr George Brewes, thus laying the foundation for his famous kennel of Shirley Retrievers. He set about eliminating the wavy coat and long leg feathering inherited from the setter and produced a slightly heavier version of the present day Flat Coat.

Shirley had many famous retrievers, the best known of which was Zelstone. The editor of Hutchinson's *Encyclopaedia*, Major Harding Cox wrote of him that he had been universally accepted as the Adam of the breed. Champion Zelstone proved himself adept in the field and to prove that his offspring were as well able to hold their own on the show bench as in the field Mr Shirley purchased several breeding bitches. From one of these matings emerged a dog which was unbeaten in show and unequalled in the field. This was the immortal Champion Moonstone. Major Harding Cox believed that all champions of the breed in 1930 could trace their ancestry on either side of the pedigree and sometimes on both.

Gordon Stables published his book *Our Friend the Dog* in 1889 and said of the Flat Coat that it was 'in general character and style not unlike a small Newfoundland very much refined, but had a longer head and not so much breadth of skull. The coat was not so massive but more glossy than the water dogs'.

The litters bred to Shirley's Flat Coats were sold all over the country and in the records the names of certain dogs appear with regularity, among them Lord Redesdale's Champion Blizzard and the Kent County cricketer Mr L. Allen Shuter's Champion Darenth, the latter being in direct line of descent from Champion Moonstone. It is Champion Darenth (1888–1900) who is responsible for present day breed lines and was the sire of Major Harding Cox's well-known Black Cloth who, although he had lost an eye due to an encounter with an antagonistic cat, nevertheless became a champion. Black Cloth was mated to Black Paint, and the ensuing litter of seven puppies contained Black Drake who founded an important branch of the Flat Coat tree of descent. Another of these puppies came into the ownership of Mr H. Reginald Cooke and succeeded in beating his litter brother Drake when they met at Crufts. This was Wimpole Peter who was not nearly as impressive as his brother as a stud dog; whereas all Black Drake's litters produced at least one puppy which achieved top honours (often they excelled both on the bench and in the field), Wimpole Peter did not manage to pass on to his progeny his own excellence.

Mr Reginald Cooke's importance to the Flat Coat breed cannot be too highly stressed because Flat Coats today would have been very much the poorer without his interest. Born in 1860, he lived for ninety-one years until 1951 and during this time his kennel, with the Riverside prefix, was the most well known name in breeding for the majority of the seventy years he was associated with the breed. He was actively concerned with showing for over sixty years and in that time gained 349 Challenge Certificates. He made up two dual Champions, Toby and Grouse of Riverside and thirty-two other Champions, keeping precise records of his dogs which included pedigrees, press cuttings, photographs and letters, all put together in beautifully bound volumes dating from 1903 to 1950. The Breed Society owns nine of these volumes and extracts from them are very often to be found in the Flat Coat yearbooks e.g. 73, 74, 76, 77 and 78. They are of unique interest to all Flat Coat owners and breeders giving much information that is of help in tracing the history of the breed. For example, Cooke states Champion Darenth weighed about seventy pounds (31.8 kilogrammes) which was considered to be over the average for the breed at that time, so that we can deduce that the early Flat Coats must have been considerably smaller than our present day examples of the breed.

The foundation of the Retriever Society in 1900 saw the first mention of a dog of a colour other than black. This brown Wavy Coated bitch was named Rust and belonged to J. H. Abbott, a gamekeeper, who won the official field trials in the October of that year where, according to Charles Eley, the critics of the breed commenced their rumblings. This was the first indication that the liver colour of a Flat Coat was acceptable. By 1918, at the end of the First World War, the Labrador had overtaken the Flat Coat in the popularity stakes and before the end of the 20s the Golden had pushed the breed into third place despite brilliant successes in the field by Dual Champion Grouse of Riverside and a bitch called Meeru owned by Colonel Weller.

Letters on the decline of the Flat Coat dominate the early part of the Cooke records and one of the theories he expressed regarding the fall from favour was the lack of style compared with the Labrador. It was at the turn of the century that the breed suffered several attempts to improve it when various outcrosses were used, some taking a long time to eradicate. One of these examples was that a few breeders decided that the dog's face should be lengthened in order to facilitate retrieving large game such as hare, and according to Major

Ch High Legh Blarney.
One of the most famous of all Flat Coat Retrievers, owned by
Mr H. Reginald Cooke. The painting is by Maud Earl and shows
Blarney holding a grouse.

Sh Ch Betty of Riverside.
The name Riverside stood for some of the very best in Flat Coat
Retrievers, owned by Mr H. Reginald Cooke, who was one of the
leading breeders and authorities on the breed in the 20s and 30s.
(Hutchinson's Dog Encyclopaedia, *photograph: Fall)*

Harding Cox this was the reason why a cross mating with the Borzoi was introduced. To the resultant progeny he gave the name 'Coffin Headed' for the offspring had long narrow heads and weak muzzles. This was a most unfortunate digression and took a very long time to breed out before the damage could be repaired, but this too was a factor that contributed to the breed's decline in popularity.

The years between 1914 and 1945 saw inter-breeding between the Labrador and the Flat Coat. Many of the resulting litters can be found in the Kennel Club Stud Books as field trial winners because it was in the period between the two World Wars that the Flat Coat, although losing its place as first favourite of the wealthy shooting men, was taken over by the gamekeepers who recognised the dog's inate ability and sporting instincts, and bred for that dual purpose performance for which this breed of Retriever is particularly famed. During the 30s the main Kennels to the fore were those of W. J. Phizacklea's Atherbram dogs with their main rival the Flat Coats of Mr W. Southam's 'Sp' breeding, who had prefixed all his dog names with these letters. Southam went out of the breed in 1937 leaving the field clear for Phizacklea to experiment with his breeding programme, particularly in the field of the liver colouring in coats. Champion Roland Tann became the first liver champion in the late 40s owned and bred by Mr E. Rowlands.

During the Second World War the breed nearly became extinct for a number of reasons, not the least being that many of the gamekeepers were called up for national service. If it had not been for such enthusiasts as Phizacklea, Cooke and others including Mrs P. M. Barwise's Forestholm dogs and the Claverdon Kennel of Dr Nancy Laughton, the breed might have been lost forever, for they continued breeding, albeit in a very restricted manner. At the end of hostilities many of the former devotees returned from active service including such men as Stanley O'Neill of Pewcroft fame (*Dog World* breed columnist for many years), Major H. A. Wilson whose Nesfield Kennel in Northern Ireland produced some wonderful field workers and of course those men who were the backbone of the Society pre-War – the gamekeepers, of which the most important, without doubt, was Colin Wells and his famous 'W' dual-purpose bred dogs who are still in contention today. Colin Wells originally founded his Kennel in 1933 and began again in 1945 with Waterman (Atherbram Simon × Atherbram Meg) who became an outstanding champion and winner in the field.

Many other names spring to mind including the late Jimmy Boyd, who was in the main responsible for keeping up the Scottish end of the breed, and whom I well remember meeting on my first visit to

A handsome quartet.
Miss Phizacklea with four of her Atherbram Retrievers, all of which
were prize winners in the 1930s. A very similar type to some of those of
present day breeding.
(Hutchinson's Dog Encyclopaedia, *photograph: Fall)*

the Scottish Kennel Club Show in Kelvin Hall, Glasgow in the 60s, to be offered a 'wee dram' from his hospitable flask. His home bred dog Monarch of Leurbost came into possession of Tom and Sally McComb on his death and became a full champion several times over before they lost him recently.

From the end of the First World War to the present day, a period of nearly seventy years, the name that is associated with the breed in the immediate post-War period was that of Stanley O'Neill, who made a great contribution and stimulated the breeding programme as it slowly gained momentum, gathering many new supporters in the process. As the breed became better known and the old enthusiasts guaranteed show classes, the issue of Challenge Certificates was kept up. One of the problems with showing a Flat Coat was that there was a shortage at this time of knowledgeable breed judges, for many of the all-rounders who officiated at these early shows leaned heavily towards either the Labrador or the Setter types and the Flat Coat is not an example of either. However, as time went on these judges were in the minority and our breed has emerged true to a recognisable type, although there are variations in such things as head and size. Since the war the number of breed registrations have risen steadily but it is difficult to know exactly the actual numbers of puppies born in the latter half of the 1970s due to repeated alterations in the methods of registration by the Kennel Club. The figures have become somewhat distorted, for not all puppies were registered by breeders and transferred from the basic to the active lists. During the 80s however, there has been a distinct upward trend, not only in the numbers of litters bred and puppies registered but also in the membership of the Flat Coated Retriever Society.

It is not feasible for lack of space here to name the Kennels founded after the Second World War whose dogs have gained considerable fame, but mention must be made of Pat Chapman's legend in the breed, the late Champion Shargleam Blackcap who, having taken the Supreme Award at Crufts in 1980, went from strength to strength winning sixty-three Challenge Certificates in total, a number of groups at Championship Shows and siring many prize winning offspring, thus bringing the name of the breed into the public eye. Most of the modern Kennels are holding on to the ideal of dual purpose work/show dogs and many Flat Coats are once again figuring in field awards. In 1980 the breed had its first English Field Trial Champion made up since before the Second World War. The Hon Amelia Jessel qualified Field Trial Champion Werrion Redwing of Collyers for her working title, at the time there being two others both owned by Major H. A. Wilson in Northern Ireland. These were International Field Trial Champion Hartshorn Sorrel and Field Trial Champion Nesfield Michael. It would be a great pity if the breed were ever to lose the working side due to indiscriminate breeding which would provide the means for a split into two distinct types of Flat Coat, namely the show dog and the working dog; in many other gundog breeds both types look totally dissimilar.

The Hon Mrs Amelia Jessel and FY Ch Werrion Redwing of Collyers, winners of the Flat Coat Retriever Open Stake in 1978.

Sh Ch Vbos Velma showing Flat Coat conformation (dam of two champions, granddam of three). Owned by Miss V. Ogilvy Shepherd. (Photograph: Frank Garwood)

An example of a typical Flat Coat head.
Ch Rase Rumaigne, May 1982. (Photograph: Anne Roslin Williams)

2

Flat Coat Confirmation

Although the breed has received a great deal of publicity since the 1980s top win at Crufts, the Flat Coat Retriever is still one of the lesser known gun dogs, and generally people still have a tendency to stop and inquire your dog's origin, or pass pointed comments on those funny-looking black Setters. It is nice though, on the rare occasion when the dogs are recognised as Flatties, when people reminisce about the Flat Coats that used to be in their family, especially in the years between the two World Wars which might be said to have been the heyday of the breed. If one looks at old pictures of the Flat or Wavy Coated Retriever, apart from a tendency for those dogs to be heavier in build than the specimens of present day breeding, there is not a great deal of difference generally. This is due to the fact that each breed has a standard which is officially laid down by the Kennel Club and agreed by the individual Breed Societies, setting out the points of a good specimen. The Flat Coated Retriever breed standards were first drawn up in 1923 and have since been slightly amended at various times, the latest standard being in 1985. They all begin with Croxton Smith's description of the general appearance of the dog. He describes it as a bright, active dog of medium size with an intelligent expression showing 'power without lumber and raciness without weediness'. In character it is generously endowed with natural gun dog ability, optimism and friendliness demonstrated by an enthusiastic wagging tail plus a confident and kindly temperament.

HEAD AND SKULL
The head should be long and nicely moulded. This moulding is characteristic of the breed. There is a gradual tapering from a moderately broad flat skull towards the muzzle, there being a notable absence of cheekiness. The change of level between the line of the skull and muzzle should be slight, giving a minimal amount of drop or 'stop'. In fact the face is fairly well filled in between the eyes which are set widely apart. The muzzle should be long although not necessarily equal to the length of skull as formerly. It should be strong, with the capacity of carrying a heavy hare and possess large

open nostrils for easy scenting, and well braced lips to obviate the collection of feathers. The teeth should be regular and ideally show a complete scissor bite, the upper teeth closely overlapping the lower teeth, but a level bite should not be unduly penalised, as should be an under or over-shot mouth.

EYES
Should be of medium size, dark brown or hazel (defined as reddish brown) with a very intelligent expression. A yellow or gooseberry eye is a decided fault as is a round or prominent one, and the eyes should not be obliquely placed. The lower eyelids should not be so slack as to favour the collection of foreign bodies in the field.

EARS
Should be small and well set on, close to the side of the head.

NECK
The head should be well set in the neck, and the latter should be reasonably long and free from throatiness, symmetrically set and obliquely placed in shoulders sloping well into the back to allow of easily seeking for the trail.

FOREQUARTERS
The chest should be deep and fairly broad, with a well defined brisket, on which the elbows should work cleanly and evenly. The legs are of the greatest importance, the forelegs should be perfectly straight with bone of good quality carried right down to the feet and when the dog is in full coat the legs should be well feathered.

BODY
The fore-ribs should be fairly flat showing a gradual spring and well arched in the centre of the body but rather lighter towards the quarters. Open couplings are to be ruthlessly condemned. The back should be strong and the loins short and square.

HINDQUARTERS
Should be muscular. The stifle and hock should not be too straight or too bent and the dog must neither be cow-hocked nor move widely behind; in fact he must stand square and move true on legs and feet all round. The legs should be well feathered. He should move straight with drive and fluency.

FEET
Should be round and strong with toes close and well arched, the soles being thick and strong.

TAIL
Short, straight and well set on, carried gaily but never much above the level of the back. Should be well feathered.

GAIT
Free and flowing, straight and true as seen from front and rear.

COAT
Should be dense, of fine to medium quality and texture, flat as possible. Legs and tail well feathered. A good dog at maturity shows full furnishings to complete his elegant appearance.

COLOUR
Black or liver only.

WEIGHT
In hard condition should be between 60 to 80 lbs for dogs and 55 to 70 lbs for bitches.

HEIGHT
Dogs 23–24 inches. Bitches 22–23 inches.

TEMPERAMENT
Confident and kindly. Characterised by a constantly wagging tail.

That is the official up-to-date picture of a Flat Coat, but let us look a little more closely at these breed points in the order in which they are stated.

First the head is unlike either the Labrador or the Golden Retriever as it is much longer and more finely produced with hardly any stop. The term 'stop' means a definite depression where the skull frontal bones meet those of the top of the muzzle, the nasal bones being raised on either side above the level of the eye sockets. The eyes themselves are set widely apart in the side of the head and should be as dark brown (not black) as possible. I cannot think of anything I should less like to see than a light-eyed Flat Coat and as Major Harding Cox says in his article for Hutchinson's *Encyclopaedia* in 1934, 'a light eye is objectionable, a yellow one fatal'.

The lower parts of the cheek are called the 'flews' and these should not be flabby but fairly tight, so the dog can pick up cleanly. In this aspect Flat Coats are unlike the Setters who tend to be a bit jowly. Earlier attempts at breeding produced a much broader headed dog than is at present popular, and Dr Nancy Laughton in her book *The Review of the Flat Coated Retriever* comments on work done by Smythe in his book *The Conformation of the Dog* as to the relation of size of head to intelligence, both coming up with the idea that it is quality not quantity of the old grey matter that counts. A Flat Coat does not want too 'snipey' a head either, but one that is balanced and looks right (neither too broad nor too fine) for the size of dog it adorns.

The ears of a Flat Coat are about five and a half inches long and fall softly on to the cheek, making useful eye wipers in times of emergency. I love to see baby Flat Coats when they are born – their little ears stick flat back to the head, inside out, like tiny warning triangles.

The head should sit on a long neck. Major Harding Cox used the term 'well moulded' which I think is very apt. Certainly a short-necked Flat Coat would look awful as it would make the dog look out of proportion and the head would be carried badly, thus throwing out the front action (movement of the fore-legs). The chest should be deep, coming out in the front like the prow of a ship to form the point called the brisket (or breast) from which the legs emerge on either side, giving plenty of room for freedom of movement because they are set back from the point of the shoulder, thus putting the elbows well under the body to allow them to work 'cleanly and evenly' as per standard.

The front legs are important because here the amount of good bone should produce straight, well-feathered limbs that can stand up to a hard day's work on round tight feet. As with a horse the saying 'no feet, no horse' is very applicable, and a splay foot does not act to cushion shocks as do the thick strong pads of the correct type of foot. When standing, a dog should be well up on his toes so that the pasterns are tight and well off the ground.

The Flat Coat's body should be well ribbed up (meaning the ribs being well separated), with a deep chest providing plenty of heart room and space for the lungs to develop stamina and wind capacity. The body should not be barrel-like but have the length and depth needed to give a typical Flat Coat 'racy' appearance. The Standard says that 'Open couplings are to be condemned'. The couplings are the space between the last back rib and the stifle on both sides and should not measure more than four inches according to Harding Cox, but certainly the stifle must be slightly bent to provide the

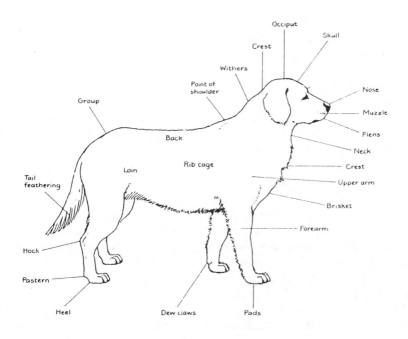

Points of the dog

correct angle for the body to stand square on the ground; the usual term is 'a good turn of stifle'.

The topline, as it is known, should be straight, producing a good level back going into nicely rounded quarters that are strong and well muscled to provide the propulsion so necessary in a gundog while working in cover. To help in this the hocks need to be 'well let down', which means they are placed low at the right angle, pointing directly at you when viewed from behind and set off by the tail which should be of a reasonable length to balance the dog, held on a level with the back. A tail which is held high is termed 'gay' and is a fault. One of the Flat Coat's most pleasing features is the ever-waving motion of a feathered plume, and to see a ring full of Flat Coats at a Show with all tails waving is a sight of which I never tire.

There are several types of coat to be seen on Flat Coats today but the correct one is that which shows feathering, is smooth and fine in quality, lying as flat as possible with a dense undercoat, the top coat carrying the glossy jet black sheen which is a combination of correct feeding, full health and good grooming. A Flat Coated Retriever's coat is made to protect the dog in thick cover and produces an oily

15

secretion which prevents water from getting to the skin. The two colours allowed by the Standard are black and liver though numerically the latter are very few. My personal preference is for the black because it is very difficult to get and keep a decent shine on a liver coat as the dogs seem to be out of coat for ten months of the year. Very occasionally a golden-coloured dog has cropped up causing much concern. Dr Nancy Laughton had one in a litter born in 1968 and some more cropped up in England and Australia in the early 80s which is why the colour stated in the Standard is so definite.

The new Standard states that the weight shall be from 60 to 80 lbs for dogs and 55 to 75 lbs for bitches. In 1934 in the Hutchinson's *Encyclopaedia* article Major Harding Cox gives the height at the shoulder for a dog as being 23–25 inches and for a bitch 19–22 inches. Since then ideas on size do not appear to have altered a great deal though many people, including myself, prefer an animal slightly on the smaller side because it is more compact. The modern Standard gives 24 inches maximum for dogs and 23 inches for bitches.

Looking at earlier recorded heights the average size seemed to be on the maximum of Harding Cox's guide-lines, but people working the dogs found the bigger dogs at a disadvantage at field trials when put against their old rival the Labrador, and began breeding them down a little. Whatever the size of the animal a dog must look like the male and the bitch the female of the species. I do dislike seeing a 'bitchy dog' or a 'doggy bitch'.

I must mention the Flat Coat temperament which is one of its most noticeable attributes and deservedly so. As a breed these dogs love people and will allow even small children to do what they will with them, even to ride on their backs or sleep in their beds, but they will guard their owners' property and although they are not fighters they can give a good account of themselves if they have to. They really do make the most loyal and affectionate companions and if you add to this their beauty and intelligence, it is not surprising that this particular dog is becoming better known. Do remember Flat Coats are big dogs given to boisterous behaviour if allowed to give rein to their natural exuberance and they do need a firm hand in training. If you are not sure how to go about it then get expert help. It is to be hoped that nothing we do will spoil this delightful old breed for the future.

3

Breeding with your Flat Coat

These days when the demand for bitches far outstrips the supply, one might be forgiven for wondering how it is that in the last fifteen years the requests for dogs has dropped so convincingly in favour of the opposite sex. Perhaps it is because more people wish to try breeding a litter, and certainly that is one of the most satisfying aspects of dog keeping, providing an interest and giving the breeder and the purchaser of the resulting puppies great pleasure and satisfaction.

In the old days it was very often thought that a bitch ought to be bred from for health reasons, otherwise she stood a chance of developing a condition known as pyometra, which is septicaemia of the womb. This can be fatal if not diagnosed in time and operated on. This operation usually entails a hysterectomy. In modern times the use of wonder drugs, antibiotics and modern veterinary science have alleviated a great deal of the danger from the condition. Also, it is not only maiden bitches that suffer from pyometra as it can affect bitches that have had litters. In our own case my Champion Rase Rumaigne had five litters, and then we nearly lost her from what turned out to be pyometra at the age of ten.

Most people buying a Flat Coat bitch usually wish to breed in order to supply all their admiring friends and relations with a similar dog to theirs. Certainly an adult Flat Coat when fully mature excites a great deal of admiration for its inherent good looks and aristocratic bearing but perhaps I might be forgiven for being a trifle biased!

It is therefore of the utmost importance that the bitch you buy for use as your first brood bitch be as good an example of the breed as you can find, for although the dog plays an obviously important part in the mating, it is from the bitch that the most recognisable qualities come. So, it behoves you to use as a brood as good an example of a Flat Coat possible, physically and mentally sound, neither nervous nor aggressive and pleasing to the eye. Some people think that the bitch is of secondary importance to the dog but nothing could be further from the truth, and to breed good stock you must use a good bitch. If you are lucky, the puppies so produced will be of such quality that you will make your name as a breeder, and should you decide to keep a bitch puppy, enable you to start the cycle all over again.

Bitches can only mate when they are in season, which happens in domesticity twice a year – in the wild a bitch would only come into season or oestrum once, in the spring of the year. They are in this condition for around three weeks at a time, although this can vary according to the individual bitch. The first season occurs when the bitch is between six to twelve months but again it can vary with the individual. You may possibly not notice the first sign of a season as it is a swelling of the vulva, but the second stage when the bitch begins to drop blood you probibly will, although some bitches are very clean and wash themselves thoroughly. Tell-tale signs can be left on bedding and on the floor, this is called 'showing colour' and counts as the first day of the heat proper. This coloured discharge goes on for twelve days or more, when it turns colourless and it is usually after this stage when a mating can take place. The bitch usually indicates her readiness for mating by turning her tail aside and this reflex can also be gained by the breeder when rubbing the bitch above the tail, which proves quite a good indication of readiness should there not be any other dogs around. If more than one bitch is kept they are likely to mount each other when they are ready and of course if a dog is kept, one is not usually left in any doubt when this is the situation. As we keep a mixed pack, we are not left long in ignorance when a particular bitch is at her peak for the dogs go into a frenzy of expectation and tear round the place, noses to the ground. They very often go completely off their food as well, this condition lasting for about three days or until crisis point is over.

When your bitch comes into season, it is usual to notify the owner of the stud dog you have chosen so that arrangements can be made in plenty of time for her visit to him. This could be a moveable feast for the day on which the actual mating can be achieved could be anywhere between the ninth and seventeenth day, but having said that I have known bitches to stand on the fourth and twenty-third days of their season, so you can see that there is no hard and fast general rule. I find that my bitches all seem to follow the same pattern and are ready to stand for the dog at around the sixteenth or seventeenth day which is fairly late. Most people take the twelfth day or thereabouts as an indication of readiness. Owners sometimes ask what is the best age to mate their bitch and I can only say that I do not consider a bitch to be sufficiently mature in her own growth until she is at least two years old and that usually coincides with her third heat. I think that a bitch should certainly have had her first litter by the time she is three, although I have known bitches of five produce and rear successful first litters, but as in humans the older the mother the more the added risk. As a general rule, one litter a year per bitch is sufficient and a maximum of five should be the limit, some breeders believe that the first three litters are the best and they therefore will not breed with a bitch beyond this.

Another question that is always cropping up is the choice of a stud dog and this is not easy to answer, for it occasions most breeders a great deal of thought. Perhaps the breed is lucky not to be as popular as some, so there is not the same temptation as in the numerically strong breeds to use a dog from down the road. You need to consider that the dog you choose should have a complimentary pedigree to that of your bitch and the same forebears are allowable as long as care is taken not to mate too closely. Very close mating such as brother and sister, or father and daughter is known as 'in-breeding' and this is not advisable. However, one can mate grandfather to grand-daughter which is sometimes done in order to perpetrate a particular trait or good point and this is known as 'line breeding'. The action known as 'out crossing' means using any suitable dog from outside one's own pedigree. It is important that you like your choice of stud yourself, because otherwise you may not be attracted towards the type of puppies he is going to produce, which rather defeats the object of breeding a litter in the first place. There is a very wide choice and your decision will be made depending on whether you wish to breed primarily for show, work or pets. When thinking about the choice of stud, a particular dog might catch your eye because of his achievements at shows or in the field and it is certainly easier to sell puppies sired by a well-known dog, as generally the dog's owner may have enquiries from prospective customers which he or she will pass on to you. This is a great help if you are just starting to make your name as a breeder. It is thought by some people that if they keep a stud dog of their own it will save them paying fees for the service of somebody else's and also make them a little money if other people wish to use him, but, and it is a big but, your dog has not only to appeal to prospective stud users but needs to be seen winning before people will consider using him as a sire.

Although opinions differ, it is my contention that dogs should be around the age of eighteen months before they are used at stud for the first time, because once they have had the experience they tend to be keener when bitches are in season. It is advisable, if possible, to have an experienced bitch for his first attempt as two maiden (unused) animals together could well achieve nothing, although in Flat Coats this is unlikely. It is better if neither the dog nor the bitch are fed before mating and it surely is unnecessary to say that they both need to have relieved themselves. Do remember that if you are taking your bitch to the dog, as is usual, it is better not to wait till you arrive on his doorstep before letting your bitch out to make a puddle, for obvious reasons.

When both animals meet for the first time, it is usually on a lead in case the bitch snaps at the dog, but once introductions are over, slip the leads off and let your bitch be free to conduct the matter in hand to her own satisfaction, for she needs to be relaxed and at ease before she will let the dog mount her. When this happens, that is, when she allows the dog to climb up, the serious business of mating can take place. It is important that a stud-dog owner knows his own dog, for some will allow you to help by guiding in the penis and some prefer to do it on their own. However, most breeders help the dog by supporting the bitch under the loin. In the meantime the owner of the bitch usually holds the animal's head in case she tries to snap or move away when the dog enters her, for this can be painful in a maiden bitch.

If the bitch persists in snapping at the dog and refusing to stand, consistently sitting down, she may not quite be ready and there is no point in allowing the dog to wear himself out to no avail. It is best to leave it until the following day and try again. If this too is unfruitful you have the choice of two options, you can either allow the bitch to say 'I don't like you and I wish to have nothing to do with you', in which case she may fancy an entirely different dog and mate without any difficulty, or you can forceably restrain the bitch and allow the dog to cover her. Again, this is to some extent a matter of knowing your animal, for bitches do have their likes and dislikes. I remember this particular point being illustrated very strongly by my bitch Pandy (Rumaigne) whom we wished to mate to Teddy; she was just not interested in having him anywhere near her at any price. Each time she firmly sat down, telling him in no uncertain fashion just what he could do with his overtures. It was a different story when we changed over the dogs and brought out Sambo. The mating was accomplished in two seconds flat, for he had sired her previous litter and she was obviously one of the faithful kind. I tend towards the view that if the bitch will not mate normally there could well be something wrong, at least in Flat Coats. But some bitches can be difficult and if it is thought that fear is the cause of her not standing a muzzle could be tried made out of bandage or a tie if the proper thing is not available.

Providing all goes well and the bitch will accept the dog, he will probably mount her several times before beginning to thrust. The stud owner will know whether his dog will allow him to help him into the bitch or whether he can manage perfectly well on his own, some dogs will come off the bitch immediately if attempts are made to guide him. I am a great believer in letting instinct do the guiding and would only help if I had to, which has not been necessary with our stud dogs who seem to manage perfectly well on their own. It is worth mentioning that if a dog doesn't appear to be trying to thrust it may be that he has a psychological hang-up. This happened in the case of our Rase Teddy, who had been pulled off bitches when he shouldn't have been there so often by me in the early days, before he was considered old enough to play at being a big boy, that when we really did want to use him at stud I couldn't understand why he was making no attempt to thrust. It crossed my mind that having been stopped so many times previously he might think that he shouldn't perform completely this time. I rang a friend of mine who is very experienced and got her to come and take over the mating and the deed was accomplished before I was barely across the yard.

When mating has taken place there occurs what is called the tie. When the dog reaches his climax his penis swells and neither the dog nor the bitch are in a position to release themselves. It is at this time that the dog pumps the sperm into the bitch. Great care must be taken that the bitch does not struggle to pull herself free because this could damage the dog, so it is important that the owner of the bitch holds her firmly to avoid this, whilst the dog is turned round. When mating has been accomplished, the animals turn back to back while tied and although some dogs are adept at sorting themselves out, others need help to put one foreleg over the bitch's back so that both are on the same side, then the hindleg lifted over so that they end up in the right position. They can stay like this from anything from ten to fifty minutes, although twenty-five is about average, until the penis goes down and the dog is able to withdraw.

As you can appreciate, you may have quite a long wait while all this is happening, so it is a good idea to have a box, bale or seat of some sort handy, as after a while you tend to have cramp from sitting on your haunches for any length of time. Be alert to frustrate any attempts by either the dog or the bitch to lie down, although it is most likely to be the latter who will try and this can result in serious damage to the dog. However, this enforced wait provides opportunity seldom available for a 'natter' about doggy happenings.

While they are tied, try to avoid touching the bitch in the vicinity of the tummy as this can prevent the dog's semen flowing down. Because there may be no tie it does not necessarily mean that the mating has been unsuccessful. I had a mongrel dog once who was as quick as greased lightning, never tied to my knowledge, and from the claims to paternity had a hundred per cent success record as far as we can ascertain. When the dog comes free he will begin to lick himself and really needs no further attention, although some breeders like to give a drink of milk or even egg and milk, for he will probably require some sort of drink afterwards. A sensible owner will pay attention to his bitch if he desires puppies. It may be old-fashioned but I always 'wheelbarrow' my newly-mated bitches, that is I hold them up by the hind legs and gently shake them. I do not know whether or not it has the desired effect, but it may prevent a rush of fluid coming away containing the semen. Therefore do not allow your bitch to relieve herself, but put her back in the car to be quiet while you have a much needed cup of coffee.

It is at this time that the stud fee should be paid, if this is the arrangement, for the fee is due for the service not the resulting litter. The cost of the stud fee varies but at the time of writing is around £100. Another method of payment is to allow the stud dog owner choice of what is called 'pick of litter', but these details are arranged between the two of you when the request for service is made in the initial stages. Should you not get a satisfactory mating (for instance no puppies are produced) it is usual, but not obligatory, to get a free return to the dog, but this is another point that needs clarifying before the mating takes place.

Before mating a bitch I always take a swab as a precaution at the beginning of the heat when I wish to put a bitch in whelp, for no amount of service will produce puppies if the bitch has the condition known as streptococci. This is quite common, particularly if your bitch is shown a lot as they seem to pick it up off the benches, and is the main cause of failure to conceive.

At the time you pay the service fee remember also to obtain the signature of the stud dog owner on the Kennel Club form to register the litter, which you should take with you on this occasion. You will need this form in order to register the litter you will hopefully be getting, and there is on it a declaration which must be completed requiring besides the stud owner's signature, the dog's registered name, number (or stud book number if relevant) and the date of the mating.

The owner of the bitch should be careful of the animal even though she has been mated, for she can still be 'got at' unofficially at this time and it has been known for a bitch to produce a family one day and then another the following or even two days later, but this is unusual. However, in order to prevent any mistakes, it is up to the owner to make sure she is kept out of harm's way until she finishes the season. There is one advantage in mating early in that the bitch, if she has held, usually comes off heat quite quickly once she has been to the dog.

About three weeks after mating it is sensible to worm the animal, and I usually start mine on an additional vitamin supplement such as Canovel or Vetzyme, but do not in any circumstances change the diet. Vets think that this is very important as it is considered to be an early cause of aborting the fertilised cells. The pregnancy usually lasts for sixty-three days or nearly nine weeks and normally the bitch starts showing her condition between the fifth and sixth week. Sometimes there are other signs that she has held before that, for she may become slower and a little more sedate, or she may change her normal habits or become more choosy with her food, all indications that she could be in whelp. It is often very difficult to decide whether she is pregnant or whether she is having a false pregnancy. Some bitches carry their young very high up in the rib cage and one is left guessing right up to the last minute. In fact there have been cases of vets stating that a certain bitch was definitely not pregnant, to be confounded a few days later when confronted with a fine litter of healthy puppies. It is possible to feel the whelps at three weeks if you are very experienced but after that, short of having an X-ray, it is not possible to tell and the latter course is not to be advised because of possible radiation effects on the unborn puppies.

About a month after mating, increase the bitch's food intake with an occasional raw egg in milk for added protein. The food at this time needs to be plenty of good meat whether tinned or butcher's, plus things like fish, rabbit and chicken with biscuit meal in addition. If a complete food is given, use one such as Wilson's Meal which contains all the vitamins necessary for the bitch's condition. If you usually only feed once a day increase that now to twice, but do not give a lot of rich food that she is unaccustomed to because this can upset the bitch, which is the last thing you want at this stage.

She should of course receive daily exercise which is very necessary, but it should not be too violent nor should jumping be encouraged, so shooting bitches need to be excused working duties after the first four to five weeks. I tend not to enter my bitches for shows if they are due on heat and I want to mate them, because they are more likely to pick up any stray virus and the show plus the travel makes them very tired.

At about the sixth week the bitch will begin to change, her body will get rounder and her teats become more prominent producing milk towards the end of the pregnancy. A decision will have to be made as to where the whelping is to take place so that the bitch can get accustomed to the place before the delivery. This is a matter for individual owners who are guided by their own circumstances as to whether the puppies are born in or out of the house. We prefer to

23

TABLE SHOWING WHEN A BITCH IS DUE TO WHELP

Served Jan.   1 2 3 4 5 6 7 8 9 10 11 12 13 14 15 16 17 18 19 20 21 22 23 24 25 26 27 28 29 30 31
Whelps March 5 6 7 8 9 10 11 12 13 14 15 16 17 18 19 20 21 22 23 24 25 26 27 28 29 30 31 1 2 3 4

Served Feb.   1 2 3 4 5 6 7 8 9 10 11 12 13 14 15 16 17 18 19 20 21 22 23 24 25 26 27 28
Whelps April 5 6 7 8 9 10 11 12 13 14 15 16 17 18 19 20 21 22 23 24 25 26 27 28 29 30 1 2

Served March 1 2 3 4 5 6 7 8 9 10 11 12 13 14 15 16 17 18 19 20 21 22 23 24 25 26 27 28 29 30 31
Whelps May   3 4 5 6 7 8 9 10 11 12 13 14 15 16 17 18 19 20 21 22 23 24 25 26 27 28 29 30 31 1 2

Served April 1 2 3 4 5 6 7 8 9 10 11 12 13 14 15 16 17 18 19 20 21 22 23 24 25 26 27 28 29 30
Whelps June 3 4 5 6 7 8 9 10 11 12 13 14 15 16 17 18 19 20 21 22 23 24 25 26 27 28 29 30 1 2

Served May   1 2 3 4 5 6 7 8 9 10 11 12 13 14 15 16 17 18 19 20 21 22 23 24 25 26 27 28 29 30 31
Whelps July 3 4 5 6 7 8 9 10 11 12 13 14 15 16 17 18 19 20 21 22 23 24 25 26 27 28 29 30 31 1 2

Served June 1 2 3 4 5 6 7 8 9 10 11 12 13 14 15 16 17 18 19 20 21 22 23 24 25 26 27 28 29 30
Whelps Aug. 3 4 5 6 7 8 9 10 11 12 13 14 15 16 17 18 19 20 21 22 23 24 25 26 27 28 29 30 31 1

Served July 1 2 3 4 5 6 7 8 9 10 11 12 13 14 15 16 17 18 19 20 21 22 23 24 25 26 27 28 29 30 31
Whelps Sept. 2 3 4 5 6 7 8 9 10 11 12 13 14 15 16 17 18 19 20 21 22 23 24 25 26 27 28 29 30 1 2

Served Aug. 1 2 3 4 5 6 7 8 9 10 11 12 13 14 15 16 17 18 19 20 21 22 23 24 25 26 27 28 29 30 31
Whelps Oct. 3 4 5 6 7 8 9 10 11 12 13 14 15 16 17 18 19 20 21 22 23 24 25 26 27 28 29 30 31 1 2

Served Sept. 1 2 3 4 5 6 7 8 9 10 11 12 13 14 15 16 17 18 19 20 21 22 23 24 25 26 27 28 29 30
Whelps Nov. 3 4 5 6 7 8 9 10 11 12 13 14 15 16 17 18 19 20 21 22 23 24 25 26 27 28 29 30 1 2

Served Oct. 1 2 3 4 5 6 7 8 9 10 11 12 13 14 15 16 17 18 19 20 21 22 23 24 25 26 27 28 29 30 31
Whelps Dec. 3 4 5 6 7 8 9 10 11 12 13 14 15 16 17 18 19 20 21 22 23 24 25 26 27 28 29 30 31 1 2

Served Nov. 1 2 3 4 5 6 7 8 9 10 11 12 13 14 15 16 17 18 19 20 21 22 23 24 25 26 27 28 29 30
Whelps Jan. 3 4 5 6 7 8 9 10 11 12 13 14 15 16 17 18 19 20 21 22 23 24 25 26 27 28 29 30 31 1

Served Dec. 1 2 3 4 5 6 7 8 9 10 11 12 13 14 15 16 17 18 19 20 21 22 23 24 25 26 27 28 29 30 31
Whelps Feb. 2 3 4 5 6 7 8 9 10 11 12 13 14 15 16 17 18 19 20 21 22 23 24 25 26 27 28 1 2 3 4

Normally a bitch will carry her puppies from sixty-two to sixty-three days but she can go three days to a week more or less than this time giving no cause for alarm. The table set out above should therefore be taken as a general guide and not as a rigidly fixed timetable.

have our litters in the house where we can hear and see them easily, but it does depend a little on whether your bitch is normally used to being kennelled or sleeping indoors. If it is the former arrangement she will probably be better having her litter outside.

The whelping quarters must be light and draught free with an electric point nearby in order to plug in an infra-red or other heat lamp. Although opinions do vary on the advisability of infra-red lamps, winter Flat Coat puppies usually need a great deal of heat and are what is called in my part of England 'nesh' or soft. A bed in a barrel is not for them if you expect the litter to survive. The wooden whelping box needs to be raised off the floor an inch or so but not so much that in the early days the puppies could fall out and roll underneath. For lining the box there are several excellent proprietory brands of a special type of bedding available these days with trade names such as 'Vetbed'. This is made of nylon fur backed with polyester and allows the damp to drain through it on to the paper underneath, while remaining warm and dry on the top. It is machine washable, non-toxic and flame resistant and a marvellous rug, but you do need at least three for they need washing at very regular intervals. Another method of keeping the box warm is to line it with two or three layers of polystyrene ceiling tiles and the puppies' body heat does the rest. That old stand-by newspaper is really by far the most practical lining for the bed. It can be disposed of once whelping is over and is easily replaceable during the eight weeks before the puppies go off to their new homes. You will find that puppies very soon choose a particular spot for their puddles but piles are a different matter. You will be surprised at the amount of newspaper you need, and although we collect throughout the year friends' supplies are always very welcome if we have two litters in close succession.

It is important when constructing a whelping box to make sure that it is big enough for the bitch to be able to lie comfortably stretched out on her side, which in practical terms means her length measurement plus half again. The width needs to allow for her height at the shoulder plus about six inches (15.24 cm) so the measurements of a box for an average Flat Coat should be about 30 × 40 inches (72.2 × 101.6 cm) in size with three of the four sides measuring 18 inches (45.7 cm) and the other at least half that so that the puppies can get in and out. It is a good idea to put a rail or a flat piece over the sides of the box so that the bitch cannot lie on any puppy that has got away from the rest of the litter. Another temporary measure is to crumple newspaper to form a pad round the sides of the box. Depending on the time of year, a heat lamp of some sort may be needed and this should be adjustable and at a height so that the warmth can be regulated for the age of the puppies. Too much heat is equally as bad as not enough and can lead to dehydration in the litter; if you watch your bitch she will soon tell you if she is too hot by panting and moving out of range.

When a bitch is mated the first thing to do is calculate the date that the litter is due, for you need to be ready for the happy event at least a week before the sixty-third day, as the family can arrive either before or after it without any undue harm. Flat Coats seem to whelp on the early side rather than late in my experience. If she goes more than two days over her time it is advisable to give the vet a call, although retrievers have been known to produce a litter up to a week late without any ill effects.

In the period of time running up to the start of whelping the bitch's temperature rises, a fact which you won't know unless you take it, but other more noticable signs are that she will probably go off her food and may start ripping up paper or digging enormous holes, for her instinct is to make a bed. You must watch her carefully at this time because if she is anything like our old Sweep (Woodwren) she would get under our big shed to commence digging. Luckily we always managed to get her out before delivery commenced and blocked up all the ways underneath but I had nightmares of her having a litter we were unable to reach, and believe me there were one or two close shaves.

I wonder why bitches usually choose to start whelping in the early hours of the morning as they invariably do. Mantling about, getting up and down restlessly, panting a lot and being unable to settle, they usually follow you round like your shadow. Do watch them carefully because in the main they have their babies very easily. I remember our bitch Pandy on one occasion, having followed George into the stables where he was mucking out, suddenly produced her first baby with hardly a change of expression. Some bitches do make remarkably little fuss and if you are watching all you see is a ripple all down the body followed by a thrust, and there on the paper is the wet membrane bag containing one black shiny Flat Coat baby. Another bitch may strain for some time before achieving the same result but if she goes on for any length of time with no puppies being produced you may have a breech birth (puppy presented wrong way on) and your vet needs calling out quickly. Puppies first see the light of day (or more usually night) in a water filled bag which the bitch opens with her teeth, biting the umbilical cord in the process, she then proceeds to lick vigorously at the tiny object (they weigh about one pound at birth) causing it to squeak and forcing air into its lungs.

It never ceases to astound me at the absolute instinctive reaction of the newly born pup, who, once it is out of the bag, squirms round in search of mum's 'milk bar' proceeding to latch on to a teat drying off in the process, while mother gets on with delivering the next one. Usually the bitch can open the bag herself instinctively, but it is important that the puppy's head is clear as soon as possible, so she sometimes needs help, particularly if another arrival comes on the scene in quick succession. This sometimes happens in the early part of the whelping when the bitch often has several quite quickly after which the rate of arrival slows down. Times of production varies from ten minutes to two hours between the delivery of each puppy but there is no hard and fast rule. The new mother may like a drink of warmed milk or may even get up and go out into the garden, but it is as well if it is dark to take a torch in order to make sure that she does not dròp a puppy en route. If when whelping the bitch is very restless, some breeders remove the early puppies to a box on their own either under the lamp or with a hot water bottle, but if you do this do make sure the bottle is well covered and is not too hot. I don't usually do this as my bitches tend to get a bit agitated if I remove the pups but I do make sure the whelping bitch doesn't bury any of them while delivering another. If you get a dead one try and remove it without her seeing you, otherwise you could well find it

Gulliver. (Photograph: David Dalton)

back in the box with the live ones. The bitch eats the bags in which the puppies are born and also the afterbirth and this is quite natural but may lead to dark coloured faeces for a day or two.

Litters vary in size from around five to twelve, but eight is about the usual average. It can be difficult to know when the bitch has completely finished whelping but usually she lets you know when she should be taken out to relieve herself, while the puppies are placed on a vetbed under the lamp if you are using one, and the soiled paper is removed by someone else and a fresh bed put down. It is a good idea to wash her vaginal area in warm water before letting her back with her babies when she will lick them all very industriously thus stimulating bowel and bladder movements. Some people ask the vet to check that mother and babies are doing well but personally, although the vet is a friend, I try not to have him come anywhere near a new litter just in case of infection. The bitch may have a slight discharge for a day or two but this can be sponged away if necessary.

Once the puppies find the milk bar and latch on to a teat the only sounds one should hear should be contented squeaks. If there are any more prolonged noises like a mewing, for example, it usually means that they are cold, hungry or ill in some way and the vet must be called. The bitch may not have enough milk, it may not be rich enough or it may even be infected, and any sign of diarrhoea is serious for it quickly leads to dehydration and death. If a loud squeaking is heard it generally means that one, more adventurous than the rest, has somehow got round the back of mum and is stuck there, so the rescuer needs to be at hand.

It is advisable to feed high protein foods like chicken and fish to the bitch for the first couple of days after giving birth, with plenty of milk, an occasional egg and extra vitamins in powder or pill form.

It should not be long before the puppies settle into a routine and to start with the bitch will probably only leave them for short periods just to obey the call of nature, but as they get older the periods she spends away will get longer. The puppies will open their eyes at about a fortnight and then they begin moving about. I usually start my puppies on solids at this point commencing with one feed of Farex increasing to two fairly quickly, and adding a tiny bit of minced beef taken off the finger, so that by the end of the first week of mixed feeding they are having two milk feeds night and morning with minced beef, eggs, fish or chicken in the middle of the day. By the age of one month the puppies are having four or five meals a day, two or three of milk and cereal although by now Farex will have given way to human foods like Weetabix or Readibrek and one or

Earlsworth Black Angel with Earlsworth 'E' litter.

two of meat or fish mixed with a very fine puppy meal. Some people give each puppy a separate dish, a saucer is ideal in the beginning, other people put two or three puppies on to one big dish but a lot depends on the size of the litter. The amount of food needed depends to a large extent on how much milk the bitch is producing and whether she will allow the puppies to go on feeding indefinitely. Again some people believe in weaning the puppies and taking the bitch off, but I don't because to produce good bones weaning must be started early and mixed feeding, combined with the dam's milk, to my way of thinking produces the best results. Certainly your bitch will not lose so much condition if the feeding burden is taken over by you. In the early stages one must make sure that all the puppies get a fair share of food both at the milk bar and when it comes to solids, to the extent of perhaps helping a small one to get a head start by fending off stronger ones for a minute or two. When you start the pups on Farex I advise you to wear protective clothing as your shoes and trousers along with the floor and the puppies themselves get covered in sticky goo so that they literally have to be washed after the event. It is surprising though, how quickly the pups learn to clean each other up, and mother too will gladly co-operate in the proceedings.

29

Food can be varied from about the age of a month. Pedigree Petfoods produce a specially blended tinned puppy food which is a very good meat and makes a change from butcher's meat, which can result in very loose motions. Scrambled eggs, cooked fish, rabbit and chicken (but of course NEVER the bones) can be added to the diet and all ring the changes mixed with meal. I use the small 'Go Dog' puppy pellets from about five weeks with also a complete meal like Wilsons mixed with milk. They should be keen on their food and I love to see them rushing about in the garden and on the call 'Puppies!' see them come from all directions to nose dive into the dishes.

One last word before I leave this chapter on breeding and rearing and that is on the subject of worms. All puppies suffer from roundworms, they are passed on from the dam and can in extreme cases cause the death of a baby animal and can certainly stunt its growth if not treated. Sometimes it is difficult to tell if a pup is infested for there are no outward signs of staring coat or distended tummies, but take it from me, they will be there. Pills must be given to counteract this condition either from the vet or from the pet shop which sells a palatable wormer by Canoval which when broken in half the pup can and will take without force. Do make sure that each pup only has the one pill. We usually have a system where as each is dosed he is put outside and can't get back that way so a lot of needless rushing about is prevented.

Pups are very curious and from about the age of a month till they leave home (around eight weeks usually) it is a time of discovery which can often lead them into trouble so it is important that there is always someone handy while the litter is at large in case of emergency. It is now that the different little characters emerge and one can learn a lot by watching individuals at this time so that if you are keeping one the choice should be made easier, at least in theory. Although breeders dislike losing their babies at eight weeks you can't keep them all and it is fun to see them going off with their new families to start a new life. You can always look forward to the next litter and start all over again.

4

Choosing a Puppy

As an established breeder, prospective owners often ask me to choose their dog for them but my answer is always no, they must make the choice themselves. I will help by pointing out various factors like that puppy is very active, and that one rather more retiring, but the ultimate decision must be theirs. It is very often a difficult thing to pick out one pup from a number of what appear to be identical babies, but usually one imprints itself on your consciousness for one reason or another thus making the choice somewhat easier. Occasionally one puppy will choose you and not the other way round. When we were rather new into Flat Coats in the early 60s we decided that it would be nice to breed with the dog I already had and to do that we needed a bitch, so my husband and I went along to Colin Wells' 'W' Kennel to choose a puppy from four in a litter by International Champion Donovan out of Champion Woodpoppy, both of whom were later exported to Italy. We had a good look at all the four puppies available for sale in order to make our choice but the decision was made for us by one of them attaching herself to my husband – every time he turned round there she was with her tiny tail working overtime. Our choice made for us, Woodwren became the foundation of my own 'Rase' Flat Coats and even those I show today can trace their pedigrees straight back to her.

The reason why I will not choose a dog for someone is not that I am being difficult, but human nature being what it is, in case something happened to the puppy later or it developed a fault that was not apparent at the time it would be very tempting for the owner in his disappointment to blame me because I chose it. So in order to avoid any unpleasantness I always let people pick their own dog, a case of 'you pays your money and you takes your choice'.

There are various considerations before you even get to the point of actually selecting a puppy, with a number of questions to be answered, and foremost is the one as to the sex of the puppy. How does one decide on a dog or a bitch? Dogs used to be easier to sell than bitches but nowadays the reverse is true and the latter command a much readier market for many people fancy trying their hands at breeding an odd one-off litter. People have the notion that bitches are more faithful and this old cliché is trotted out without fail if one asks a prospective purchaser why he has decided on a bitch. In point of fact this is an old wives' tale, for in my experience dogs are equally faithful, particularly with women – something to do with the affinity of opposite sexes, like a bitch being loyal to a man. In fact if someone is choosing a family pet I would advise a dog in preference to a bitch, for unless you wish to breed having a bitch is somewhat of a waste, and then there is the added problem of twice yearly heats and the unwelcome attention of all the local canine Romeos of doubtful origin that are allowed to roam at will. With a dog there are no show or shooting days lost due to being in season, although if one acquires a highly sexed dog that too can have its problems, but to be fair the Flat Coat does not usually suffer from this disability.

The second question is what colour dog do you require? This is not very difficult as the predominant gene is black and most puppies are the colour of coal. The standard also allows liver (called chocolate in Labradors but liver in Flat Coats) and some of the present day lines can trace their pedigrees back to the original one, Champion Roland Tann. There are unfortunately a few yellow puppies appearing in some lines recently but this colour is not allowable, and while no doubt they make lovely pets I feel they should not be registered, thus preventing them from being bred from. Personally I prefer the black colour for a dog, for when in the peak of condition the coat shines like silk and in fact in all the litters of Rase dogs I have had there has not been a single liver amongst them. It is often difficult to keep the coat of a liver in show condition for the sun can fade it and during the summer these dogs then have either to be kept indoors or smothered in lanolin and are really only in coat for about two months of the year.

The third question is where one is to obtain a puppy. Fortunately Flat Coats are not a big breed like Labradors or Golden Retrievers so one is unlikely to be able to buy one in a pet shop or puppy farm, but I would tell anyone to go to a breeder for your dog and preferably to an established kennel, for they guard their good name jealously and offer a proven line, besides giving help and advice in your choice of puppy. Should you not know of a breeder of Flat Coats a glance at the weekly newspapers *Dog World* or *Our Dogs* should help, or purchase a copy of *The Dog Directory* obtainable from most bookshops or Dog World.

The cost of everything has risen and with it the cost of puppies so I can only give an estimated price at the time of writing. Most breeders base their costings on how much money the litter takes up for food, Kennel Club documentation, electricity, vets fees, telephoning plus the cost of the stud fee which is something in the region of £75–£100 according to how well the dog has done in the field or show ring. In 1987 puppy prices averaged out around £160, and contrary to most peoples' expectations that does not leave a very big profit when one takes into account all the hours that go into whelping and rearing a litter that cannot be charged for if the asking price is not to be prohibitive.

When people come to me for a Rase Flattie I ask so many questions that they must compare it to the third degree! I have been told by friends who started off as purchasers that it was quite an intimidating part of the whole procedure, but when I have reared my puppies and watched them grow over the past eight weeks, they have developed their own personalities and I hate parting with them. I must be satisfied that puppy and prospective owner are right for each other, and thàt the latter can supply exercising facilities and room to keep a big dog who likes to be part of the family. As a general rule I will not sell to flat dwellers or members of the forces although I have done so if they are going to stay in one place for three or four years, either in this country or abroad. At the time of writing I have a dog with the Army in Germany, just starting a second four-year tour of duty, having gone out first aged twelve weeks. Nor will I sell to people I dislike, but luckily that does not occur very often and many people who have come to buy a puppy have become in time some of my closest friends. Again, I will think very hard about letting a puppy go to people who are out at work, for it is most unfair to take a pup away from the companionship of the litter into a strange environment, let alone one where he is completely on his own for hours at a time. Breeding a litter has its funny and sad sides but some people hate the moment of parting so much that the trauma is sufficient to put them off ever having a second mating.

One of my early questions to anyone enquiring about the availability of a Rase pup is 'what do you want a Flat Coat for?' Far too often the answer is 'only a pet' which is a pity as these dogs are dual purpose bred in the main. Even today it is still the proud claim of the breed that it is just about the only work/show retriever left and obviously to be able to work the same dog as one shows can only be an advantage. Some kennels have a name for work and others for show, but whether you require a puppy for one or the other the dog you buy should be able to do both jobs and also be a pet as well. A Flat Coat is an active, intelligent canine and being a pet is not enough, it really does need some form of discipline to harness all its surplus energy and as a member of a gundog breed that is obviously the most natural outlet for training. Whether you want to show in

33

Earlsworth Blackbird (Merlin) 8 weeks old.

beauty, obedience, or work to test standard, or take your place with the shooting élite at field trials, you need to choose a kennel whose breeding programme produces puppies best suited to your particular requirements. Like all of the long established kennels I have a waiting list for puppies, so anyone requiring one in a hurry may not be lucky and will have to either go somewhere else or contain their soul in patience. It is nice if having ordered a puppy the buyer can watch it grow during those first eight formative weeks by paying visits to the litter at regular intervals, but this is often easier said than done as Flat Coat breeders are still not very common and are dotted around the four corners of the country. I like to keep my puppies till around eight weeks old as I feel they need the security of the litter till then. I don't take the bitch off for she will stop them herself when she wishes, so by this time they are being supplementarily fed four or five times a day. They will not be getting much of the dam's milk by this time anyway, but I consider that as it is the most natural food they may as well continue for as long as possible, for it all contributes to a sound extrovert puppy, able to take the new experience of changing houses in its stride.

As I said at the beginning of the chapter, I don't offer advice on the actual choosing of a puppy for I think that is a personal thing, but there are several pointers that should be borne in mind when making a choice from a litter. The first is that ideally you want a playful, strong, bold pup who comes rushing up to receive his share of the fuss that he knows comes from those odd, two legged creatures who bring his food at regular intervals. He should be compact and sturdy with good bone and tight feet. His bright eyes should be dark, with an intelligent expression, set in a head that has a long moulded line along the muzzle that is neither too broad across the skull nor too narrow across the nose to make him look snipey, and the ears should be neat. His tail should be well set on level with his back and the puppy should look balanced. The coat should be dense, shining clean and quite flat; there should be no scratching, which would indicate fleas or lice, which are not to be encouraged, and the typical equable Flat Coat temperament should be well to the fore. If you are lucky you may be able to see the sire as well as the dam, the latter is usually very much in evidence and very proud of her family, thus it is possible to gain some idea of what the puppy will look like when he is mature. At the age of eight weeks the puppies should be exhibiting signs of working ability, picking up things in their mouths, and they will be delighted to fetch a ball or a toy thrown by you to demonstrate their retrieving instinct.

Having made your choice of puppy from the litter and paid the

Kodak with the bitch Eskmill Bamboozle and their litter.
(Photograph: David Dalton)

asking price you should receive in return a diet sheet showing on what the puppy has been fed and times of meals. It is fairly traumatic for the puppy to leave behind all that he has known from birth to go to a completely new environment, without the added problem of changing his food which could bring with it diarrhoea and an upset tummy. In addition to this sheet you should receive, if you are lucky and the breeder has applied early enough and the Kennel Club computer performed satisfactorily, a flimsy sheet of paper which is what passes for a registration these days, with the official name of the dog and his KC number written down for all time. Do make sure that the breeder has also signed the back so that transfer of ownership can be affected. Along with this you should also have a signed copy of the pedigree, which traces the pups relatives back usually for five generations, and which it would pay you to read, mark, learn and inwardly digest, so that when another Flat Coat owner asks 'how is he bred', you don't give them a blank stare and ask what they mean. Some people do find a problem in understanding a pedigree but it is not difficult if you remember that the sire's line is always on the top and the dam's on the bottom, with their parents, grandparents and great grandparents forming a horn-like structure, the apex of which is your pup. When talking about your puppy's breeding it is usual to say that he is 'by' whichever dog is his sire, 'out of' (or written down it looks like 'ex') the dam or bitch who had the litter. It is my contention that although of course the dog is important (well, you couldn't really do without him as artificial insemination is not allowed in England yet) it is the bitch who has the strongest influence on the puppies, because it is often possible to get an idea of how the pups will mature by studying the conformation of the dam.

On the pedigree you may find certain abbreviations which look rather baffling so perhaps I had better list them for you in order, to enable you to interpret the family tree of your puppy.

JW is Junior Warrant, which is not an official title, but means that before the animal was eighteen months old he won sufficient first prizes to total 24 points for which he was awarded a certificate.
Ch means Champion. I usually show them in red on my pedigrees. It means a dog or bitch which has gained at least three Challenge Certificates under three separate judges, and in gundog breeds has passed a test of working ability on actual game.
Sh Ch is a Show Champion only, in other words has not yet qualified for the working award. It is considered as a lower ranking than a full champion and owners of the above are encouraged to drop the 'Sh' as soon as possible. To that end the Society holds an annual qualifying stake for show dogs to enable them to do this.
Int Ch stands for International Champion. This means the dog has gained titles in two or more countries, which is difficult to do in England as Ireland is the only country to which one can take dogs and bring them back without the dreaded quarantine restrictions. Occasionally English Champions are sold abroad and can also gain their titles in one or more additional countries.
FT Ch is the most highly prized of all the titles, for it means Field Trial Champion and is gained by the difficult feat of winning three field trials. These are stakes run over two or three days with shot game, for which you need Lady Luck on your side in large amounts.
Together with the above, the initials *FTA* can sometimes appear alongside names on a pedigree. This indicates that the dog was

placed in Field Trial competitions and explains that the dog was a good enough game worker to receive an award at the high standard required by these official trials. Do not confuse Field Trials (held with actual shot game) with working tests where only dummies are used.

If you are taking possession of your puppy at the usual age of eight weeks, he will be too young to have received any injections in the main, although there are a minority of vets who advocate early innoculation against such diseases as parvo virus. Certainly the puppy will have little immunity to such diseases as hard pad and distemper, the old scourges of the canine world, along with the more modern leptospirosis (which can cause jaundice symptoms) and yellow jaundice. He will have some immunity from his dam, but should not be taken out in public places until he has received the usual jabs at twelve and fourteen weeks. There are some advocates of innoculating puppies at about a month old with a type of measles vaccine, but it has been found than this can lead to complications later in life and I would not recommend it. If your puppy is over fourteen weeks when you get him, remember to also obtain the signed vaccination booklet showing the brand of serum used and the date for the booster, usually twelve months ahead.

Make sure also of the last date of worming and when the next treatment is due because this is most important; worms can cause the death of baby animals if they are not treated properly. There are all sorts of products these days, the most recent ones treat the bitch during pregnancy and prevent the infestation of the whelps, which in the past have all been infected by roundworm via the dam, but as yet I have not tried this method. Tablets can be obtained from the vet or from the local pet shop but make sure you obtain the roundworm and not tapeworm treatments, for the latter attack animals over six months whereas roundworms cause puppy infestation.

These days many breeders offer an insurance cover note on the puppy for a nominal sum, to take effect from the moment you leave the kennel premises. It covers the animal in case of death from illness or disease, loss from theft or straying and veterinary fees among other things, and remains valid for six weeks. After this the insurance can be continued by payment of a further premium.

Pedigree Petfoods produce a folder with all sorts of leaflets on feeding, training and so forth and I always like to give my purchasers a copy along with the other paperwork.

Having chosen your dog, paid your money and received your documents, you are now free to embark on the adventure of bringing up your Flat Coat puppy, which requires a certain amount of knowledge, a certain amount of common sense and last, but not least, a sense of humour!

5

Puppy Rearing

One of the advantages of starting off with a puppy rather than a partly grown animal is that you can bring it up the way you want it to go, by commencing training at an early age. Owning a dog is a serious committment and when a puppy first arrives to become a member of his new family, he can be very bewildered by the change, although most adapt fairly easily. However, the process is complicated if the puppy is given as a Christmas present, when he could get too much or too little attention in the general fracas during the hectic period of the penultimate week in December.

The organisation known as PRO-DOGS produce a car sticker which states 'A DOG IS FOR ALWAYS NOT JUST FOR CHRISTMAS', in an effort to try and impress the importance of dog ownership on people contemplating giving a puppy to a child as a Christmas present. So many of these well-intentioned gifts unfortunately find their way to dogs' homes soon after 25 December, as their new owners discover that a baby animal is not just a toy to be picked up and then discarded at will, but something that requires almost constant attention. Most reputable breeders therefore refuse to sell stock at Christmas unless they know something of the environment into which the puppy is going. The reason for this policy does not take much looking for; there is so much excitement around at the festive season, particularly on the part of children, that live presents in many cases tend to be overwhelmed if common sense is not brought to bear. I prefer to let puppies go off to their new homes without any extra complications, so I will not sell at Christmas; that way the youngster and his new owner have a chance to adjust to the change in their lives. Flat Coated Retrievers are very adaptable and settle down pretty quickly with their new owners. They have been called the canine Peter Pan because they never seem to grow up and even when they are getting on in years they still retain their sense of humour, to say nothing of their tail waggers record. The breed is very outgoing, one might even say extrovert, for they are certainly not backward in coming forward to greet anyone calling at the house. Indeed, one of the first problems as the dog grows up is how to curb the exuberance, complete with a broad grin, which manifests itself in general by jumping up at everyone who comes to call.

The temperament of Flat Coats is one of their greatest assets, they love to be with people and enjoy being fussed by all and sundry. They are as gentle as lambs with small children, whom they look after with all the innate intelligence of the breed, but they guard their territory, warning of strangers with a deep bark that puts off the unwanted caller in no uncertain manner. I think that there must be a sign outside our place warning gypsies not to call, as we very rarely get visits from what used to be called in the old days 'Hawkers and Circulars'. But let us not put the cart before the horse. First the new puppy has to be reared successfully and as I said at the beginning of this chapter, common sense goes a long way, and if coupled with a little knowledge most of the teething problems can be ironed out in a relatively painless operation.

Having collected your puppy from the breeder the first thing is to get it home as easily as possible. The ideal situation is to have two of you in the car; one to drive and the other to nurse the pup because although he may start off in the back of the vehicle, it will not be long before he has clambered forward to the nearest lap and that can be somewhat disconcerting, especially if you are trying to drive round and through a wriggling Flat Coat. Do remember to take plenty of newspapers and a towel because the pup could be affected by the car's motion and be sick on the journey. Some are and some are not, there does not seem to be any hard and fast rule. In my own case I have only ever had one dog that was car sick, and time and patience in taking him everywhere soon cured that. These days the problem is at the other extreme for my dogs prefer to jump into the car and stay there just in case I take off somewhere without them.

Having survived the journey home and had a sniff round his new abode, the first job is to feed the recent arrival as it is probable that he has not had any food for several hours. The breeder would probably only have fed him if there was sufficient time for the meal to be digested before travelling, in order to avoid sickness, or alternatively the puppy could have emptied his stomach en route. Either way he is likely to be ready for a meal, after which he needs to go out into the garden to relieve himself and then be shown where and in what he is to sleep. I will take each of these three factors and discuss them separately.

First feeding, and any breeder will tell you that good bone results from good food; you must put the goodness in to achieve the results of a strong, healthy adult dog. Although the breeder will have started the process it is up to you to continue the good work, for these early

41

days are very important. By the time the puppy leaves the litter at seven to eight weeks old he has been on four feeds a day for several weeks. The feeds are usually spaced out around breakfast, lunch, early and late evening time. Along with this his dam was probably still available for the odd tipple at the milk bar when he could catch her standing still long enough, because by this time she was probably all but running dry. So when he goes out into the wide world he is dependent on what you, his new owner provides. Some people advocate only feeding one of the complete foods, which admittedly is far easier in time and thought than traditional methods, but I think from the amount of nose twitching that goes on when there is something special on our menu like chicken or rabbit, a dog is similar to a human and is interested in eating different foods. Although complete meals are all scientifically balanced they are very dull and prosaic and as food is the highlight of a dog's day it is nicer to vary the offerings each time. Breakfast is usually some form of cereal such as Weetabix or Readibrek, depending on the time of year, along with milk. At this time I also often use a proprietory 'complete food' such as Wilsons, Valu-mix or Dual, mixed with hot

Feeding time in Denmark.
Danish puppies at 5 weeks. Jiggers Blackbird × Dan Ch Van Dango Chianti (DOB 13.3.85). Owner/breeder Christin Buus Christensen.

or cold milk. The best milk is goat's milk which can be obtained frozen before the litter comes along and a stock laid in. I also use cow's milk in liquid or powdered form but it does need to be the full cream variety. It is also possible to use evaporated milk mixed with water to dilute it, or calf or lamb starter, and I have used out-of-date baby milk from the chemist, so there are infinite possibilities. It is quite a good idea occasionally to mix in a raw egg and a spoonful of vegetable oil (like one uses for cooking) which helps to keep the coat looking shiny.

Lunch, at roughly one o'clock, is usually a meat and biscuit meal of sorts and I use best mince from the butcher, Pedigree Chum Puppy Food, a roll or chubb of brawn in various flavours, or dried meat soaked in oxo, though too much dried meat can cause scouring so it needs to be mixed with a biscuit meal of some sort, or mixer such as produced by Pedigree Chum. To the meat I add puppy or small terrier meal, any vegetables available such as greens or potatoes and mix thoroughly. Occasionally, if not using dried meat, I add a warm gravy, but do remember a pup does need to get his teeth into something hard in the food line in order to produce strong white teeth.

About six o'clock another protein meal is produced, to vanish down ravening throats almost without touching the sides. Scrambled egg, fish, chicken, rabbit or soya morsels are again mixed with biscuit or mixer meal, which is sometimes enlivened with a little grated cheese. I usually give milk after lunch and often after the early evening meal, and of course there is always plenty of cold fresh water available as it is surprising how much puppies drink if given the chance.

The last meal of the day occurs in our house somewhere between ten thirty and midnight, depending on how involved I am with whatever I am writing and how insistent the big dogs are for their supper. In the case of the puppies this is another milk and cereal effort plus some small biscuits like Biscrox or baby Bonios, again to encourage the teeth. Access to a good raw bone of some size with which they can really come to grips is also important for teeth. Another food to try is tinned rice pudding, like the evaporated milk this is often cheaply available from the pet shop in unlabelled tins, and helps soothe an upset stomach if a pup gets the scours. Another tip for the scours is the water in which rice has been boiled or the addition of cornflour to the food.

Dogs are like people and require varying amounts of food so it is a matter of trial and error in the quantity involved for your puppy, but the rough guide is to allow three-quarters of an ounce (or 21·3gm) of solid food daily (that's not including milk or gravy) to start with, and increase the amount commensurately as the animal grows and his intake capacity improves.

Now to the second factor, that of training your puppy to be clean. When he leaves the breeder he is likely to have had more chance of realising that he must relieve himself outside rather than inside the house if he was a summer puppy, because it is so much easier when the weather is pleasant to encourage the right habits than in the cold and snow of January or February. It is important that you, as the new owner, adopt a sensible attitude towards this element of training. People who buy 'Rase' dogs always say they have very little trouble in this direction and this is because as soon as it is possible around three weeks of age, and weather permitting, I feed outside so that they can then relieve themselves as a matter of course and it becomes a habit. Dogs are normally clean animals and even when blind in the nest will come away from the rest of the litter to make a puddle (that is why the floor of the box should have some part left uncovered by the vetbed or blanket so that the newspaper can be used for their toilet). This use of newspaper can be utilised to advantage if the weather is sufficiently inclement as to mean the meal time must be indoors, as the puppy can be encouraged to perform on newspaper put down near the door.

Unless the garden area where the pup is to go is securely fenced so that he cannot get out, it is not very intelligent to put the puppy out by himself as he could get into all sorts of mischief. In a contained area, if you are within earshot, he can explore for himself without restriction. If this proves to be impossible, one way out of the dilemma is to have a moveable pen made of chain link fencing in which to shut the puppy, but it is important to remember that young animals can catch cold if left on damp grass, or become overheated in the hot sun, so shade and water must be provided for the periods after play when they sleep for lengthy periods.

After a meal the puppy must be put outside and often they will respond to a phrase such as 'Hurry up' and learn to perform to order. Usually it is in the same place and the droppings can be picked up and either put in a chemical dog loo or buried to act as manure. It becomes somewhat of a chore however when you have quite a number of dogs and then the picking up can be almost a full time job! A youngster can pass a motion several times during the day, because of the vast amount of food intake in comparison to a mature dog, and will also spend a number of 'pennies' so he needs to be put out at regular intervals. Always put him out after sleep and food but also in between, thus avoiding puddles or worse in the

A Rase Gladiator × Romantic Mist puppy.
Sometimes I just sits and thinks.

house. Do remember that puppies are only babies and have a very small bladder so they need to relieve themselves constantly. If there is a mistake in the kitchen, for example, it is your fault because you did not put him out soon enough. It is cruel to rub his nose in the mess; praising him when he gets it right will have much more of the desired effect. It is too much to expect a puppy to go through the entire night so it is advisable to shut him up somewhere like the kitchen, with the floor covered in newspaper during the hours of sleep. Although he may be clean during the day it could be some time before he has control of himself through the night.

I am assuming that the puppy is going to sleep indoors because that is our way of going on, but if you wish him to sleep out that simplifies matters. There are two schools of thought, one preferring the dog to be inside and the other feeling that outside sleeping quarters are better; both have valid reasoning behind them. If we take the latter first, the thinking here is that a dog is much keener to work if kept in a kennel away from other distractions, and many working men and keepers subscribe to this school. Others, myself included, feel that a dog that is a pet, companion and worker in whichever field, will work more willingly if he is always with you. It is one of those questions you, as a new owner, must answer for yourself.

We will assume you have subscribed to the indoor kennelling idea and so the next question arises, where? If you don't mind the dog in the bedroom that answers itself, but be warned, Flat Coats grow to be a fair size and if they start on the bed and then you increase your numbers, you can soon find that there is not much bed left for you, so it is better to train the puppy to sleep in his own bed rather than on yours.

The alternative is somewhere like the kitchen so the pup can be confined to that part of the house, but in the first instance, having been summarily plucked from his brothers and sisters, he is liable to be a very lonely little dog and will object loudly to such treatment. You will have to harden your heart and stick it out, for if you weaken and take the puppy in with you the battle has been lost and you may as well give up the idea of leaving him in the kitchen for good. Two pups together alleviates this problem as they keep each other company, but it is not everyone who can afford, or cope, or have space for two boisterous Flat Coats. Usually the pup will complain at first and then settle down, but there are always exceptions to any rule and our first little bitch, Sweep, was just such a one. Having chosen my husband as hers she did not intend to be parted all night and after two and a half sleepless nights, when we had tried a loudly ticking clock, the radio on all the time, cuddly toys, a hot water bottle and so forth, I gave in and deposited her on the bottom of the bed at my husband's feet and we all fell into an exhausted sleep. She slept there every night of her life except in the first couple of weeks of nursing her litters.

I advise new owners not to put a puppy straight into an expensive new basket or dog bed because little teeth can wreak havoc on cane or canvas. It is much more sensible to get something like a cardboard box that can be discarded and replaced as its use wanes. It needs to be off the floor in winter, especially if the latter is stone or concrete, but this is not so necessary during the summer months when the pup may lie on the floor where it is cooler. I line the box with a blanket or equivalent and underneath that I put one of the square sample pieces of flooring like warm cushion vinyl that are sometimes sold off (very cheaply) by our local supplier, or alternatively carpet squares that do almost as well in preventing the cold from rising. The box must be large enough for the puppy to lie comfortably and will need renewing as the animal grows, which they seem to do at a tremendous rate. It is during sleep that they grow, so children must be taught to leave the baby alone while he is in his bed, for he does need somewhere to retire to for undisturbed rest. Young dogs, like children, require varying amounts of sleep; some can do with a little while others need a lot. I understand it is something to do with the time of birth but cannot vouch for this fact. There is one other proviso, if there is a solid fuel boiler where you are planning to leave your dog to sleep, do make sure his bed is well away as there have been cases of the fumes accidentally poisoning dogs.

The choice of dwelling for the outside dog varies. It is possible to obtain de luxe model kennels as a ready made complete unit with house and run, a far cry from the old idea of chaining up a dog on guard, such as most farms did in the 'bad old days'. If you can afford the expense, it is not such a bad idea to invest in one, because then the puppy can be trained to stay in it while you are out, leaving the house and its contents intact and safe from damage, which must be a consideration these days, and of course the puppy is safe and out of harm's way.

It is possible to save the cost of specially made housing and convert part of the garage or a shed, but the area must be dry, light, airy and draught free. It is also important that there is a flow of fresh air as only recently a number of dogs were killed because they were shut up in an airless kennel during a heat wave. Should you be considering increasing the numbers of the breed you keep, it may be worth going to the trouble of concreting a larger area than you need initially, because then it will be ready when you come to extend the kennelling at a later date. Do make sure that the occupants of the kennel are able to receive a fuss from visitors, for a Flat Coat is a sociable animal and hates to be left out of whatever is going on.

It matters little which way you decide to keep your dog as long as he is warm and dry and receives plenty of exercise and human company. A Flat Coat will get used to either house or kennel but remember they are friendly beasts who ask nothing better than just to be with you.

The question of exercise can be quite a problem, for many people do not realise that over exercising can be just as detrimental as under exercising. Too much exercise can lead to a condition known as Hip Dysplasia which affects the hind movement and in the worst extreme causes lameness and great pain, so exercise with a little caution and a lot of common sense. I never walk my puppies until they are six months old and then only on a lead while the others tear about round them. The necessary free running can be obtained in a confined space like a garden, and if playing with another puppy they will decide how much they need for themselves and stop when they are tired. If this is not possible it is up to the owner to play with the puppy by throwing a ball, for example, for Flat Coats love retrieving and this can be the start of working training, but there are snags as I shall discuss in Chapter 7.

That doesn't mean that puppies can't be taken out. They should become accustomed to a lead from the age of three months but walks should be very short up to about the age of eight months in order to allow the bones to set properly. Another method of exercising, should your time be curtailed, is a taut rope or wire stretched between two points along which a ring and lead is allowed to run, attached to the dog, but if on open ground don't forget the poor little dog should the sun get out or a heavy shower fall.

Perhaps here I should have a word about putting a puppy on a lead for the first time, for often it reminds me of the old fashioned term 'titting' where a young horse being broken was tied to a post, very securely (because if he got away he was spoilt for ever and could not safely ever be tied up) and encouraged to try and pull free. The antics some pups indulge in remind me of the young horse as they rear up, rush forward pulling, then come to a complete stop and try going backwards. Some, on the other hand, accept it as part of growing up with the minimum amount of fuss. If yours is one of the former, encourage the forward progression with lots of praise but don't stop walking, just keep going at a steady pace and it won't take long for the penny to drop that it is more comfortable to walk than do the other thing. Some people put tight collars on their puppies from an early age, but they should not be left on, and remember they must be let out as the puppy grows. One way of telling if a collar is comfortable is to insert two fingers between collar and neck, if you can't the collar is too tight. The dog will soon learn to accept a collar, even if in the early stages he tries to scratch or bite it off, he will soon forget he's got it on. If one has puppies regularly, as I do, then a set of varying sized collars are useful, but if as many people do, you have a pup once in ten years, it isn't worth buying one and a way round the problem is to obtain a show ring lead combining collar and lead in one. This can be bought in leather, rope or nylon, of which leather is by far the best as it doesn't cut into your hand if the pup suddenly attempts to take off.

I always say to my puppy purchasers when they collect their Flat Coat for the first time, treat him as you would a baby and you'll not go far wrong. Like a baby he will need plenty of protein, sleep and love and this, plus some common sense, will probably be adequate even if you've not been a proud owner previously. There are one or two tips which may be useful that I now pass on to you. First, when you have to give a pill (which some people find difficult), hold the top lips over the teeth and push two fingers against the bottom jaw, thus extending the mouth as wide as possible, whereupon the pill can be pushed to the back of the throat quickly and the mouth closed and held shut while you massage the throat with the other hand. Some dogs (and puppies) are very clever at palming the pill so that you think it's been swallowed but it is spat out again when you are not looking. Always make very sure it has gone by having a look under the tongue and round the gums. This is very important when giving worming pills for it is important to see that the dog ingests it. Liquids need to be administered through the side of the mouth, making sure that it is kept closed during the process or you run the risk of tipping the medicine all over yourself, which can easily happen if you are holding the puppy at the time.

There is a right and a wrong way of holding a puppy and one should also be careful when lifting puppies up. The weight of the animal must be supported underneath as it is lifted by the scruff of the neck; this isn't cruel, it is the method the dam uses when she wants to move the litter. They should never be lifted by the front legs as all their weight is on their shoulders and this is very bad for them. Children in particular need to be taught how to pick up a puppy and support the weight while it is off the ground. Lift a puppy into the car, do not tug at it from the front and be careful that it does not jar itself when jumping out as this can cause lameness, particularly in the heavy breeds like Bernese, although Flat Coats do not benefit from such treatment either. Never allow your dog to jump up to take anything held out of reach in your hand, for landing when all four feet are off the ground can jar them badly. It is a heinous crime with a gundog breed to play pulling games as one would with a terrier. Never allow the children or anyone else to tug things held in the puppy's mouth. As his jaws close and he bites the object in order to retain his grip, just think what that would do if the object was a pheasant. Bad habits such as these are inculcated in puppyhood and then cannot be eradicated, so don't allow them to start.

One of the habits I most dislike in other peoples' dogs is being a nuisance at the meal table and this need not arise if they are trained, as ours are, that meal times are for humans and not dogs. I will not allow titbits to be given at the table at any time. Any bits left over from the meal are distributed in the kitchen afterwards or put on to their dinner plates at the appropriate time. If the puppy is persistant he will have to be shut out of the dining-room while you are eating until he can behave in company. Before the present restrictions on taking dogs into restaurants came into force I well remember when on holiday one day and out to lunch we rose from the table and extricated four Flat Coats from underneath, much to the amazement of the people at neighbouring tables who had no idea they were there.

Many of the Retriever breeds are chewers, and Flat Coats are no better or worse in this direction. You may be lucky with your pup and find it has not got this fault but it is unfair to leave edible objects within reach if you don't want to lose them. One of the reasons puppies chew is boredom, particularly if they are left alone for a long time, so if you have to do this give him a good marrow bone and some toys of his own, like a squeaky animal and a slipper, and switch on the radio. It is good training for puppies to be left for a while at an early age, for they then become accustomed to it and this saves trouble later. In fact it is not a bad idea to put the dog into kennels for a night or even a weekend once he gets to about eight months, so that if you ever have to go into hospital or rush away on an emergency you are not worried in addition by the fact that the dog is in kennels for the first time, having never been left behind before. The same factors apply to leaving a dog in the car as leaving him at home, give him something of his own to chew and the chances are he will leave the padding and upholstery alone, but there seems to be no reason why one dog will chew and another won't.

One other point that is sometimes forgotten is that if you live in a bungalow your dog will have had no practice in negotiating stairs. If you are travelling by train, for example, and need to cross the bridge to get on to the other platform, you have no time to be teaching your dog how to go up stairs *and* grapple with the luggage at the same time!

Bringing up a Flat Coat needs a sense of humour plus common sense and know-how, and if you hit snags you have only to ask your breeder or any other Flat Coat enthusiast for their help in solving the problem.

6

Adult Flat Coat Management

When fully grown a Flat Coat is quite a big animal, and if a dog of this size is allowed to please himself without any restraint he can be far too boisterous. Many new owners make the mistake of not being firm enough in the early stages of training and instead of them being the boss, the dog is; a position which is not conducive to the best relationship for all concerned.

When born, a Flat Coat puppy weighs around one pound. They grow very rapidly until at about twelve months the average youngster will turn the scales at between fifty to sixty pounds, with a maximum of seventy plus at maturity (somewhere between two and four years old). Dogs (as only to be expected) are the heavier of the sexes and body-up later than the bitches (who often have a litter around the age of two). But the breed in any case is one of the late maturing ones and if you compare a Flat Coat puppy of say six months with a Labrador or Golden Retriever of the same age, the former always looks younger, even if it isn't, because it is so unfinished. Personally, I think the longer a puppy takes to reach maturity the better for its future, for a dog reaching its maximum at an early age can coarsen and is often over the top and finished by four years of age, whereas a slower maturing puppy lasts very much longer in the show ring and at four years should be right at the peak of his career.

So one is faced with an adult of around seventy pounds in weight, which can be a problem if all this power is boisterous and untrained. The breed is very prone to jumping up, and when people are wearing decent clothes they don't want a dog leaving muddy paw marks all over them. My husband often jocularly warned our visitors to come calling in dungarees and wellies to limit the risk! Small children too can be very frightened if knocked down and belaboured by a frantically wagging tail, even if only with the friendliest of intentions, so it is most important that basic obedience is taught from the word go. Flat Coats are nice 'people' but, like children, need to be taught manners or they can become a damned nuisance. Puppies need to know what is required of them from the sit, stay, heel and return to owner commands. These are the bricks on which the house is built before more advanced training can take place, so let us look at the four basic requirements individually.

It is quite simple to teach a puppy to sit if you back him up to a wall and, holding his head under the chin with your right hand, place the left on the puppy's rump and press down, while at the same time lifting up his chin and using the command 'sit'. Make a fuss of him when he complies (praise is of far more importance than anything else when training), for with the wall at his rear he cannot back away and should go down easily into the sit position. Leave him there a second or two then let him get up. Training of the baby puppy can commence as early as eight weeks as long as it is short and sweet, otherwise they become bored. The next stage should be when the pup answers to the command and a push just above his tail. The third stage should be just a voice command only. The voice plays a very important part in training and the release command from the sit should be in an entirely different tone, so that the pup knows it is free to move.

Following the command 'sit' should be 'stay', and for this you need to restrain the dog with the left hand while making a downward signal in front of his nose with your right, simultaneously using the command 'stay'. Make a fuss of the dog after he has complied, not forgetting to change your voice tone for the release from the exercise. It doesn't matter which words you use for any order as long as you use the same ones each time, for it isn't the word the dog understands but merely the association with the same sounds. The next time give the command 'stay' and the hand signal and take one step away to the side and return before releasing the dog from the sit position. When you can move several steps away without the dog following you can then try moving in front of him. You need to hold on to the lead so that if he does decide to rush off he won't get very far. Should this happen, you must go to him (never the other way round), put him back on the exact original spot as far as possible, and start the exercise again. You must watch your dog very carefully and be ready if he transgresses, the secret of proper training is to be just one jump ahead of your pupil. If the puppy persists in moving, having been told to stay, deepen your voice in disapproval and bump him down the next time. It is worth making sure however that the puppy is not getting up because he is frightened you are going to leave him behind, in which case you need to take a much more reassuring approach. The old saying 'softlee softlee catchee monkee' is very relevant here, and when he sees you are not going far but always return fairly quickly, and the exercise is done often enough, he should gain in confidence. You must make sure that any command given is obeyed once it is learnt and if the dog is told to 'sit' he must do so. If he doesn't, you must insist that he does, even if it requires the use of stronger measures, but first you must be sure he really understands the order. When you can walk round behind the dog who remains steady at the 'sit stay', you can then increase the distance between you until the ultimate goal of leaving the dog while you are out of sight is obtained.

The down is a very much easier exercise to teach, for the dog naturally adopts this stance of his own volition. Do not use the phrase 'sit down' because you are muddling the animal as the two commands require two different actions and should not be confused. If the 'sit' is required that command should be given and similarly if the 'down' is required that must be the word used. Should you wish to do obedience competition work points are lost if your dog confuses the orders. To teach a dog to 'lie' on command, the best way is to get him into the sit position and keeping your left hand on the scruff of the neck pull down on the lead, at the same time giving the command 'down' followed by 'stay'. Another way is to take both front feet in your hands and pull them forward so that the dog automatically collapses into the correct position, but whichever method is used the command 'down' should have the desired effect.

It is important that the dog walks properly on the lead. How often have you seen an owner being taken for a walk by the dog and not the other way round? Puppies should be introduced to the lead in the early stages and I usually use a leather show ring one for this purpose, for it combines collar and lead in one but is not harsh and will slip like a choke chain. In the previous chapter I wrote about putting a puppy on a lead for the first time so I will not go over it here. Having got the pup to accept the lead one does not want to go to the other extreme where he pulls and does not walk properly to heel and as this does not come naturally it must also be taught. Many novices make the fundamental mistake of working the dog on the wrong side, for it is only correct to have the dog on the left hand of the trainer. The reasons for this are that as most people are right handed it is easier to work a dog on the left of the body. Coupled with this is the fact that in the days when dogs were trained mostly for shooting the majority of peoples' gun arm was on the right.

I use a leather ring lead when teaching a puppy to walk to heel but with a stronger, older dog a more corrective method is often necessary, especially if he has been allowed to lapse into bad habits such as pulling. Dr Roger Mugford, the canine pyschologist, has recently perfected a 'Halti', which takes its name from its similarity to a horse's head collar or halter, and I understand this is most successful although I haven't tried it personally. The other method is a choke chain as advocated by Barbara Woodhouse in her training methods. Incidentally, there is a right and a wrong way of putting these on. To be correct the chain must run back freely when not under pressure, otherwise it is no deterrent to the puller.

To start off with do use a lead that is long enough, for you need to have quite a bit spare to play with, and begin with the puppy close to you in the 'sit' position. When you are ready to move off give the command 'heel' and move away at a normal walk. The puppy's nose should be at your knee and the lead slack, but obviously this does not happen all at once; it is much more likely that he will either rush forward or hang back. Your left hand should be half-way along the length of the lead and the handle loose in your right hand. Your hands in this position should give you the maximum amount of control but do make sure your left hand has the knuckles uppermost not your fingers, or you can't get the necessary leverage. A slight jerk on the lead should either bring him back from his forward impulsion or encourage him to move forward from a backward one. If it doesn't, jerk the lead more strongly, at the same time using the command 'heel'. It should not take long before the animal understands that his nose is not required too far forward, but if you are dealing with an older, untrained dog you may need to use a rolled up newspaper which does not hurt but is satisfactorily noisy, or position the dog between yourself and a wall or hedge to obtain the desired effect. The secret is always to be consistent and when on a lead always to require the necessary 'heel' position. When your dog will walk to heel without a lead you have achieved your aim but some dogs take a lot longer than others to reach this. When training, do remember that heel work is very boring, so do not do more than a few minutes training of this at a time. It is worth remembering that a dog that 'as plenty of free running exercise is much more likely to walk properly on a lead when it is necessary, than one who is only exercised under control, although another recent innovation has been the flexi-lead which the handler can pay out from a rigid handle, after the style of those running tape measures. This is very useful for those dogs who will not return to their handler when called. Obviously this should not be necessary in the case of a Flat Coat because they are always returning to see where you are, but I should think Afghan owners who daren't let their hounds loose at all must bless its invention.

All dogs need to be trained to the recall and many owners are their own worst enemies in this case. You must remember a dog's mind does not function like a human's, so if you call him and he does not at first return and then you thump him when he does for not coming sooner, it does not take a vast canine intelligence to work out that if he is going to get beaten for returning, it might be best not to go back at all. A dog can only connect cause and effect, and correction must be applied at the time or it is useless. Unless you are a sadist and use an implement to hit the animal the amount of damage you can inflict on him is negligent, you'll injure your own hands more. On the few occasions when I have needed to break up a fight by using a riding crop it upset me emotionally far more than the dogs who were soon the best of friends again. There should not be much trouble in getting a Flat Coat to return to you if he associates the coming with something pleasurable like praise, a titbit or a meal, and our puppies leave the litter in this happy state. Later, when the dog is on to a nice smell and does not want to leave it, comes the test and some owners do not help themselves by only calling the dog to put him on the lead at the end of a walk, instead of doing as I suggest and calling him several times during an outing. *Never* call a dog to you and then punish it, for you destroy its trust in you, always go to the dog to punish it. This is sometimes easier said than done, but if you can't get him back any other way use a flexi-lead and you can then reel him in and praise him for returning.

Praise is very much more effective than punishment but like a number of other breeds Flat Coats vary in their responses and can be either 'soft', when a sharp word is enough to finish them off for that training session, or 'hard', when stronger measures are required to make the point go home. In the latter case the most effective results can be gained by grasping the dog firmly either side of the neck and shaking him with feet off the floor (his, not yours!) but usually a deep tone of voice while looking into a dog's eyes is quite sufficient with Flat Coats, who are normally among the easiest of breeds to train because they want to please you. You should praise as often as possible but be careful not to over do it, especially in the case of an exciteable youngster and those dogs in whom the clown is rampant, for it can make training much more difficult. Equally as bad as over praising is the other extreme where some handlers, particularly men it seems, are too embarrassed to praise their dog in public and good work is ignored, to the puzzlement of the dog, so under praising can be as bad as over doing it.

Leaving aside the question of training let us turn to the other facets of management and here feeding looms large. I have always maintained that the idiom 'little and often' with regard to meals is the best, because Flat Coats can be subject to torsion (a twisted gut) which I am sure comes from an over-loaded stomach, so I always advise feeding adults at least twice a day. In fact my own dogs are fed three times, which is hard work for the owner but certainly brightens up their day!

To grow up fit and healthy, sound in mind and limb and with sufficient bone to carry their frame, must he the aim of your feeding programme, and Flat Coats do need a fair amount of food to do this. In the main they are sensible eaters with no particular fads and fancies, although this depends a bit on how you bring them up. Many of them are quite greedy and can run to fat if not curtailed somewhat, while others are dainty eaters belonging to 'Pharoahs lean kine' category. Of the first group I well remember a dog we sold into Grimsby who had the job in the morning of seeing the children off on the school bus. On the way back he had two or three ports of call, gaining a breakfast at each, he was not averse either to helping himself en route to cartons of cream and bottles of milk on various doorsteps, with the result that he closely resembled a young Newfoundland in shape and had to be returned to the breeder (us) for a slimming course!

A puppy is usually on four feeds when he arrives but may soon indicate he does not want one or more of these as time goes on. Some puppies do continue with the four, in which case the amount must be cut down and divided up so that he thinks he is getting more. A Flat Coat usually grows upwards till two years old and then 'bodys up' for another two, particularly the dogs; bitches seem to mature earlier, especially if they have a litter about the age of two. Like humans, a dog's food intake varies and some do genuinely need more than others, so the owner has to recognise the difference between need and greed. There are times when dogs do need more food, for example a working Flat Coat in the shooting season, or one that is often being used for stud, and of course a bitch carrying or feeding a litter needs extra protein in its usual form of meat. Normally I feed one third meat to two thirds biscuit or mixer meal plus any leftover vegetables and household scraps for one meal and the other two are of milk plus a complete food or cereals. I vary the main meal so that it is sometimes dry and sometimes wet, and the meat can be tinned or from the butcher, even dried, which is usually reconstituted with oxo or stock, or those brawn chubs which are most useful as they do not need refrigerating. There are many complete foods on the market, some containing meat, those I use are Wilsons, Dual, Valu-mix and our pet suppliers own concoction. If you give bones make sure they are not splinterable and never give raw pork as it is conducive to worms. A number of people only feed the complete products, which no doubt saves an awful lot of time but is scarcely the most exciting method as far as the dog is concerned. Yet others never feed milk, why I can't imagine, as all dogs start off on this product and if it is good enough then, it surely must be so later in life. To my mind there is far too much nonsense talked about scientific feeding these days, and many dogs would benefit by going back to the good old fashioned ways of going on.

Eating requires teeth, unless the dog is to always be fed on soft foods, and good teeth in young animals are as important as in children. When born, puppies have no teeth, in fact their mouths are shaped to suck. As they develop so the shape of the mouth changes to adapt to eating and at five to six weeks old they should have twenty-eight sharp little needles or milk teeth. These drop out naturally from around the age of four months when they are replaced by the permanent set of forty-two teeth by the age of six months. Occasionally there can be problems if the milk teeth remain and overcrowd the permanent teeth and then a visit to the vet is in order. Calcium (of which teeth are formed) can be obtained naturally by correct feeding but it is a good idea to give extra vitamins in tablets like Vetzyme or Canoval, or sprinkle a powder on the food itself, but be careful not to overdo the additives as then the dog can grow too big in size, often resulting in a coarsening overall. Like a number of other breeds Flat Coats are required to have a scissor bite which means that the top jaw slightly overlaps the bottom one (like a closed pair of scissors). If the top jaw is too far over the bottom it is called overshot or if behind the bottom jaw it is called undershot. Both conditions are bad faults and the animals concerned should not be used for breeding. A dog suffering from either an over or undershot mouth (except in the breeds where it is permissible) is unlikely to progress very far up the showing ladder.

Management also covers turning your dog out in as good a condition as possible – if you are feeding correctly, half the job is done for you as this is reflected in the shining condition of the coat. Flat Coat owners are lucky they are not faced with the hours of preparation necessary in Afghans for example, for our presentation is relatively simple. The tools for the job obviously include the basics such as a brush and comb, but to these you need to add scissors, thinning shears (which are scissors with a serrated edge), plucking knife, chamois leather and hand glove. You can also have combs of varying teeth thickness, a rake comb and other bits and pieces which need to be kept together. I use a zip pouch that started life as a soft pencil case which is permanently kept in the dog show bag so that I know where to find it. This list of equipment is likely to be more than you will require for ordinary grooming: if you do not intend to show then a good brush and comb a couple of times a week is all that is necessary, except in the spring and autumn when coat changes occur and ears, feet and feathering need pulling out. I will explain this more fully in Chapter 8 when I discuss showing your Flat Coat.

Novice owners often bath their dogs too often and this can remove the natural coat oils present in a healthy dog. It is not necessary to bath before every show and in fact I often use a dry shampoo instead of a water one. We usually bath during the summer to remove dust and such like, just before Crufts, and at other times for social or medical reasons. The former usually means that they have rolled at a particularly pungent spot or swum in stagnant water, and the latter reason is to combat a flea or mite plague which seems to occur some years far worse than others, and can manifest itself in an outbreak of flaked skin or scurf. Other conditions such as mange or eczema are treated by bathing using a special veterinary shampoo, otherwise an ordinary one is all that is necessary and there are many proprietory brands on the market. Bathing a Flat Coat is not the easiest of jobs and we generally use our own bath because of the ease of getting them in and out (although the latter does not often constitute a problem) and the shower attachment can be used so that the water is not too hot. Dogs, like children, hate soap in their eyes and the coat should be rinsed well. Sometimes in hot weather they have to go under the hose in the garden but I reckon we end up wetter than they do most of the time.

I tell my new puppy owners that if they treat their puppy like a baby – plenty of good food, sleep and love, with controlled exercise they will not go far wrong, for Flat Coats are very easy dogs to manage and provided they start off on the right foot they can only go on to improve, maturing into a dog to be proud of.

7

Working the Flat Coated Retriever

The Flat Coat has lost a great deal of the popularity it had a hundred years ago when it was the shooting dog for gentlemen. It has been superseded by the other Retrievers, particularly the Labrador, but having said that, the Flat Coat is still the only truly dual purpose Retriever out of the three (I am not considering the Curly or the Chesapeake) for the same dogs are both shown and worked. At present there are not the structural differences to be found in this breed as in the other two, when show and work strains almost look like two different dogs.

Flat Coat Retriever enthusiasts are trying hard to retain the working side of these dogs and while not everybody has either the time or the facilities to reach field trial standards, most people can train a dog to fetch a dummy and reach working test levels. A Flat Coat is a big dog which if not trained becomes very boisterous, so everyone needs at least a course of basic obedience.

It is worth remembering before one embarks on any training programme that dogs learn with the help of their natural instincts so it behoves the trainer to acquaint him or herself with their natural behaviour. The dictionary definition of instinct is 'an innate driving force' which means the behaviour of an animal without any training, as for example turning in a circle before lying down which would originally have been necessary to flatten the grass to form a bed. The instinct of a puppy to chase anything that moves has to be sublimated by training so that he will move quietly to retrieve a thrown object or shot game, yet sit and wait for the command to do so. Another instinct such as bringing back prey to the den in the wild state can also be incorporated when teaching the retrieve.

Dogs cannot reason as human beings do, so they do not understand words, only sounds. It would be possible to teach a dog to sit, lie, stand etcetera by using entirely the opposite commands, as long as the trainer was consistent in what he said. No animal can actually understand what is said to it, so it is not what is called 'anthropomorphic' despite the claims of some doting owners. A Flat Coat has a high rate of intelligence and can reason within its own limited powers, and to obtain the necessary man/dog partnership the

Rase Marmoset and Downstream Finality at work on the Scottish moors. Owned by Mrs G. Lawrence Jones.

handler must understand the way a dog's mind functions. Any dog is fundamentally a pack animal and as such needs to know the pack leader (its owner) and its place in the pecking order. Many novices make the mistake of not realising that they must be the pack leader, for in the wild there is a strict descending order so that every dog knows where it stands in relation to every other, and it is therefore actively cruel to deprive any dog of the companionship of either humans or other canines. It only takes two dogs to form a pack whereupon the group instinct rises to the fore. In the wild the pack leader is in charge and each dog or wolf takes his place in the order of things, depending on his personality. The leader is the strongest and most dominant dog, be it either male or female, and running a mixed pack I have often found that the overall leader, after myself, is a bitch. If one is to train a dog one has to act as pack leader, not only giving the orders but seeing they are obeyed.

In training one finds that dogs fall into two categories, those that are 'soft' or in other words need to be trained gently, or those that are 'hard' when often harsh tones need to be implemented by physical correction. Flat Coats are usually in the first group, although of course there can be exceptions to any rule. More often than not a great deal of praise is necessary with Flat Coats if they are not to collapse in a quivering heap after being shouted at, this is why Labrador trainers seldom understand Flat Coats and do not bring out the best in this breed. By physical correction I would suggest that in order to show displeasure at your dog's action the most effective method is to pick the dog up on either side of the neck and shake him, at the same time gazing into his eyes, for dogs hate to be stared at, while berating him with your voice. There is little point in hitting a dog for you do more damage to your hand than the animal, and apart from separating a fight I would not use an implement like a riding crop because it is unnecessary to inflict that sort of punishment. A trainer will obtain far better results by the use of praise, either by tone of voice or with his hands, for like people, dogs need to know that they have pleased you.

In addition to the natural work instinct the dog must have that innate wish to please you in order for you to get the best from him; if that is missing you just cannot make contact with the dog at all. A person who is too self conscious to praise their dog in public is as bad as those who go to the other extreme and make too much fuss, for in the first case their animals are always slightly unsure if their actions meet with approval or not. Each owner needs to know his own dog's character for some, like people, require much more reassurance. Like a child who shuts his ears if his mother is continually nagging, a dog does not listen to a stream of commands given by the handler if the gist is lost in a welter of words. Orders need to be given clearly and concisely. Do not shout, a dog's hearing is far better than ours, but there are times when he is concentrating so intensely on what he is doing that he simply does not hear voice or whistle if blown continuously, in which case it is pointless to continue. Praise or punishment must be instantaneous, a result of the dog's immediate action, for a dog cannot associate anything else in his mind. Action and result must follow as the night follows the day in order to make the association required by a dog's limited intelligence. One of the worst Flat Coat faults is 'running in' especially at working tests or in training – in other words the dog sets off to retrieve the article before the order has been given, a bad fault which will quickly put you out of the running in a competition, so it is important that the youngster is prevented from developing this fault which is often associated with over keeness. One way to cope with this is to have your dog on a flexi-lead which will pay out until stopped, whereupon the dog fetches up with a sudden jerk which should prove the necessary deterrent. The trainer must then *go to the dog* and scold him before bringing him back to the heel position. The trainer must always go to the dog and not the other way round otherwise the dog associates the return with the telling off and not the 'running in'. You have to be quick and often a word can prevent the dog rushing off in the first instance. It is worth remembering that a habit once formed is difficult to break and a little bit of anticipation on the handler's part can prevent these faults from starting. If you give an order you must see it is obeyed, for your dog must do as he is told, when he is told. If he does not you will be unable to make much progress in a training which needs basic obedience as its cornerstone.

There are some people who, though willing, will never train a dog. They just do not possess the necessary ability to make the dog obey them, perhaps they are naturally Indians not Chiefs. In such a case the dog will probably work well for someone else, only reverting to his old ways when returned to the previous handler, and there is little that can be done about it. However, assuming most people are going to attempt to train their own dogs, with some degree of

Mrs V. Kendalls' Tokeida Midnight Melody in the field.

success, it is worth remembering the following facts. Firstly, rewards and/or corrections must be given in accordance with the dog's actions and never be dependent on the mood of the handler. If you are in a bad temper do not attempt to train your dog, and certainly do not nag your dog, for he only associates direct action and response – it is no good threatening a dog for he does not understand. The only result of hitting a dog is to make the handler feel better and as the dog probably is unable to reason the workings of the owner's mind nothing is gained. When I hear people saying that they hit their dog every time he does something, but that it makes no difference, it makes me want to say to them that they are wasting their time and some other course of action should be employed. A dog that has been berated for some wrong-doing needs to be found something to do that merits praise, so that he and the handler can regain their former footing. It is important that the handler is one hundred percent sure that the dog has understood what is required of him and is being deliberately disobedient. If there is any doubt that the dog simply does not understand he must be given the benefit of that doubt, for it is no good giving an order which the dog does not understand. *Never, ever* call a dog to you and then punish him, for that will destroy any trust between you and the animal and is quite unforgivable as I have stressed before.

I have already covered walking to heel, sitting and staying in Chapter 5 on training a puppy, but another of the basic requirements is the retrieve, which can be commenced in the house at a very young age. Baby puppies from as young as a month will carry things in their mouth instinctively and this can be encouraged. Many promising youngsters are spoilt by thoughtlessness, for never under any circumstances should an article be grabbed from the dog even if it does happen to be one of your best shoes which you were daft enough to leave lying around. The dog should be called to you, praised, and his mouth gently opened and the object removed while the command 'dead' is given. The dog must associate the praise for delivering to hand and if possible the article should be returned to him. You must be consistent in your training however, for it is no good getting mad with the dog for chewing your shoes one day and then taking no notice the next when he is chewing something else. A puppy needs to learn which are his toys and therefore permissible to chew and which are out of bounds.

I am often asked what to do about a youngster (or older dog) that will not return to the handler. This really should not be a problem with Flat Coats for they are always tumbling over themselves as puppies to be first to receive a fuss and should always associate the

David Hutchison seen running in Flat Coat Field Trial with Ch Black Velvet of Candidacasa at Waverton. (Photograph: David Dalton)

return to humans with something pleasant. Should you have one that is reluctant to come back you could try running away from him. If he still evinces no interest, bend down and pretend to study a blade of grass with your back to him, or even lie down flat. When he does come up to see what you are doing, don't make the mistake of grabbing at him but encourage him to you and make a fuss of him, taking the article if he is carrying one without staring him out, for dogs do hate that. If he will not 'give' up the article *never* pull, because it only teaches him to hang on and produce a hard mouth, which is a bad fault if he presents a badly bitten pheasant to the judge for appraisal at a field trial. If he does not give the object up voluntarily, hold the scruff of the neck with the right hand saying 'no' in a firm tone followed by the command 'dead'. If he still refuses to let go on the second request and is still hanging on, tap his nose sharply. Be ready to make a fuss of him once he does relinquish the dummy and don't make the mistake of praising him for hanging on instead of letting go because you are too slow on the uptake. Like a child, a dog needs to know that 'no' means just that and not 'maybe', a dog will try you on if he thinks you are a soft touch.

Flat Coats have to be taken very slowly and often proper training is not advisable until they are over the age of twelve months, it depends on the receptability of the dog, but certainly it needs to have achieved its adult teeth. It must be remembered that Flat Coats mature much more slowly than either the Labrador or the Golden; if they are started too early they stand the chance of reaching a plateau where they have to be stood off for a while until they regain an interest in the proceedings. This may or may not occur with dogs kept in the house, but those who are kennelled rarely suffer from this as the dog is so pleased to do something when he is let out that he is raring to go, whereas one that is allowed to run loose round the house and garden is not nearly so keen. A dog needs to know when he is working and when playtime begins for obvious reasons.

The retrieve should not prove a problem with a Flat Coat but there can be difficulties occasionally. We have had one or two exceptions to deal with over the years; one bitch would not fetch anything at all until one day one of the cats fetched in a rabbit that was still warm, this she retrieved with no trouble at all and from then on fetched anything, but without much interest unless it was the real thing. Another, a dog, would only bring back articles if covered in rabbit skin, so if the retrieve is posing a problem it may be a matter of trial and error to find out what is the key to the puzzle. Retrievers must deliver to hand, which can cause problems if the dog plays about with the object just out of reach, or bolts back to his bed with the dummy. The latter may be overcome by positioning oneself between the dog and his goal in order to intercept him en route, or teach the retrieve in a narrow passage way with no other option but straight back to you. The former problem can be dealt with by controlling the dog by either a flexi-lead or by a twelve foot length of light cord. But it is very easy to get tangled up in the cord if one is not careful, resulting in a muddle of dog, handler and tangled cord, putting the dog off for good – for this reason I would only use a check cord as a last resort. Don't make the mistake of grabbing the dummy the moment the dog comes back, for that is in a way a punishment, but turn and run away as the puppy races up to you and then you can remove the dummy on the move if necessary. If the dog returns but spits out the dummy at your feet, kick it away and praise the dog encouraging him to pick it up from there and praising him when he does so. If you continue to have this problem you need to put the dummy into his mouth, closing the jaws round it and giving the command 'hold'. When you remove your hand after a

Ch Heronsflight Black Bell of Yarlaw, 1964–1973.

short while give the command 'dead' and take the dummy from him. This can be repeated until the dog himself will continue to retain the dummy until the second command is given. It is worth remembering that youngsters get bored very easily and it is often the best policy to do a few minutes training twice a day rather than half an hour at one stretch, or a concentrated session one day and then nothing for the next two, although an occasional break in training can be restful for both trainer and pupil.

The aim in the early stages is to have a dog that will wait for the command to retrieve, then travel out to the object and back to the handler as quickly as possible by the shortest route. Steadiness and directed retrieving will come later but it is important in the early stages to get your dog to fetch back willingly, for this is the crux of any retriever training. A puppy can be started off in the garden with hidden toys, gloves or a dummy and encouraged with commands such as 'Hi lost!' or 'Seek' to use his nose in trying to find them. Here of course wind direction helps a puppy for if he can get down wind of the object so much the better, therefore it is more sensible to find out the wind direction (by holding up a wetted finger) and utilising that. Be careful not to let the dog see you hide the object or he will use his eyes not his nose in locating it.

Flat Coat working at a game fair, here showing jumping ability. (Photograph: David Dalton)

Once a dog can fetch thrown dummies the second stage is fetching unseen objects. This can prove difficult and, to encourage the dog forward if he has not actually seen anything fall, it is usual to push forward with your hand and arm while at the same time moving your body slightly forward while giving the command 'get on' or 'forward', and when he is near the spot telling him to 'Hie lorst' or 'Seek'. If the problem arises when the dog will not leave you to go forward, you will have to take the dog to the object and show it to him, encouraging him to retrieve while you run away in order to receive the retrieve at a distance. Another method which might pave the way for the unseen, is to walk the dog at heel, dropping a dummy as you go and after a while stopping and sending him back for it. You could also hide several dummies close together, sending the youngster for each one separately, but try to discourage the retrieving of more than one at a time. We once came fairly high up in the results of a scurry as Kelly picked up two objects in one go and succeeded in getting them both back to me, but this practice is frowned upon at a working test or field trial and can result in elimination.

In Flat Coat training the love of water can be brought into play fairly early on and usually there are no problems at all (they come later in trying to keep the dogs out!). Occasionally a puppy might be somewhat shy but with a little encouragement they will go in with another dog or dogs. If there is no canine help available you will have to go in yourself, but make haste slowly and build up his confidence in shallow water first, preferably in a stream on a hot day in summer (you won't get a lot of choice here I'm afraid, although we do get one or two) so that no actual swimming is involved at first, merely a paddle. The dummy can be thrown up on to the opposite bank in full view and the youngster encouraged to retrieve it, this can then be made more difficult with a slightly deeper crossing which may require further immersion or even a stroke or two before regaining terra firma. If there is not a stream available, a pond or lake would do equally well providing the bottom does not shelve away so that the youngster suddenly finds nothing beneath him. The sea is quite good too, but in some places it also tends to drop away without warning. To start with, the dummy can be thrown a foot or two out on the water's surface, with the distance being increased as the dog becomes more sure of himself. If there is a current it would be advisable to have a more experienced dog standing by to retrieve the dummy should it be carried downstream, or further out. Failing that it should be possible to tie a light nylon cord to it, providing of course in all the excitement you remember to stay attached to the other end of the line! Dummies for use in water need to be able to float. They can be either the manufactured canvas ones or can be made from empty liquid washing up bottles filled with a little sand and covered with a material such as an old nylon stocking, socks or something similar. Rabbit skins can also be attached round the bottle and even pheasant's wings to introduce the pup to fur and feather.

Retrieving from water should be fun and most Flat Coats love it, taking to the element like the proverbial duck. But one word of warning over long distance water retrieving: do watch your dog carefully to see that he doesn't suddenly panic and begin frantically swimming in circles. I think they become disorientated for some reason, and often a shout from the owner has the desired effect of heading them back for the bank and averting disaster. I have known two cases where this disorientation has happened to experienced dogs: one was my own Samba who was practically within touching distance of the dummy when he began swimming in circles. By rushing round the lake yelling I got him to the side without mishap, but had I not been watching carefully I believe he would have drowned. I could never get him very far out from land afterwards. In the second case the same thing happened (both were at working tests) and the owner was so concerned he actually jumped in to save his dog and had to be pulled out himself, the dog eventually managing to make the bank under his own steam.

Poppy Mills or Rase Galliard retrieving game from water.

Training can be reinforced during every-day activities, particularly during the usual exercise period. Unless you have a large garden where the dog or dogs can run, animals need to be taken for free running exercise, off the lead, every day. If they do have a large garden, as in our own case, they need only go three or four times a week if time is at a premium, as seems to be the case in most people's lives these days. This free run can be used to encourage the youngster to use his nose in investigating the bracken, dead grass and bramble cover to follow up the various scents therein. It is also a time when steadiness to stock can be taught by taking the pup on a lead to within close proximity of cattle, horses and particularly sheep, and strong disapproval shown if any attempt to give chase is shown. If on the other hand the youngster appears frightened reassurance from the handler is very necessary.

Acclimatising a youngster to people *en masse* is also an important part of any training whether for show or work. It can often be traumatic for a puppy to go out into the big wide world with all the traffic and hustle and bustle of present day living. Puppies bred by us are reared in the house so that they are accustomed to the internal noises of living – hoovers, washing machines, television, telephone and so on – and once they have had their injections I usually take them into our local country town to acclimatise them to pavements and diesel fumes as well as humans and vehicles of all sorts. During the summer if it is not too hot, I often take them to a show of the agricultural kind where there are many new sights and sounds and hundred of people to stop and make a fuss. If you do this you must be able to leave them with a friendly stall holder or take them back to your vehicle when they get tired. No dogs should be left in a car during the heat of the day because it becomes nothing less than an oven under the sun and several dogs belonging to thoughtless owners have died in awful circumstances in this way. You can of course carry your dog when he gets tired; my champion Romulus when a baby let us know when he had had enough for he used to stop, stand on his head and then collapse in a heap, much to the amusement of Joe Public.

To teach a youngster to keep his eye on the handler in training is difficult but one of the ways in which this is done is to hide from him so that he has to use his nose to hunt for you, using only short distances at first but gradually extending the range. It can also be done by use of whistle signals but remember, if the handler is forever blowing his teeth out on a whistle, the dog, like a child, closes his ears and does not listen. Like oral commands, whistle signals need to be short, sharp and to the point. There is no need to use more than

A liver Flat Coat Warresmere Cedar, owned by gamekeeper Mr K. Butler. Winner of the Flat Coat Society All Ages Stake 1983, Olney, Bucks. (Photograph: David Dalton)

one and people who appear at tests hung about with the things are often those whose dogs are the most uncontrolled. There are two types, the silent (or very high pitched note) and the ordinary one usually made of bakelite or staghorn which I prefer as I then know we can all hear it. Actual whistle signals vary somewhat with different trainers but as a general rule one long blast is for stop, which may or may not mean sit, and a series of short notes mean return to handler, when a titbit can be given for a quick response. Teaching the pup to sit on the whistle is best taught with the animal in the heel position and the whistle is then blown every time he sits when the handler stops. This association of sound and action should imprint itself on the dog's mind so that it will work some distance away. The hand can also be raised, palm outward, so that whistle, hand and voice can reinforce the command.

Once the basic standard of obedience is obtained, and that is best done at home where the youngster can concentrate without distractions, there are two ways of training. The first is to continue by yourself, which is slightly artificial and may cause you to have problems later when you enter for competitions with distractions such as other dogs about. The second is to join a good dog club, of which there are many dotted around the country. These clubs usually run classes for puppies, intermediates and advanced dogs, so that as your dog learns the basics he can progress up the ladder to more advanced work. Regular competitions are also held in the form of Field Trials, working tests or scurries (timed retrieves) and teaches both you and the dog to work in company. The United Retriever Club is the biggest of these, while the others form the constituent members of the National Gundog Association; a list of these can be found in their bi-annual show catalogues published in August and December, when one of these clubs acts as hosts for the occasion.

I would never advise a trainer to allow a young dog to be played with by children on their own. They particularly should be discouraged from throwing things, or encouraging the youngster to jump up, or pulling any object being carried from his mouth. If they chase him around when he is carrying anything he will be much more difficult to train in retrieving to hand when the time comes to work properly. All sorts of bad habits can be set up quite unnecessarily in these circumstances.

Another warning needs to be given with reference to gunfire training, for although in the Flat Coat breed it is most unusual to find a gun shy puppy, that is not to say that there are none, and training ought to be commenced with the utmost caution. Here help is needed, the one to handle the dog while the other takes charge of the gun some way away down wind of the animal. I say gun but we always commenced in this training with a starting pistol followed by a dummy launcher before progressing to a twelve bore. But whatever weapon is used, the first shot should be into the air, well away from the dog who should remain unconcerned by it all while the handler makes a fuss of him. A second shot, nearer, in conjunction with a thrown dummy (in the opposite direction) should evince some interest, whereupon the pup can be allowed a retrieve. The shots can get closer until being loosed within a few yards of the dog, who should not show any concern but only interest in the cold game being thrown, such as rabbit, duck or pheasant. We sometimes took trainees to a clay pigeon shoot once they were steady to shot, for it is a good preparation for the shooting field proper. If however, the puppy does become apprehensive at the sound of the weapon, stop using it during the training sessions completely, and transfer to banging off during play, feeding or exercising times, when the puppy can be made much of until he eventually loses his fear of the noise to the extent of working with the gun. Some people have divided thoughts on the use of a dummy launcher, which although it can propel the dummy a long way, does so with a very loud bang, which can have the effect of putting many dogs off if they are in close proximity to the noise.

It is worth considering for a moment the accomplishment of jumping, which is often very necessary in competition retrieving. There are some very good old photographs showing Flat Coats stylishly clearing gates, often carrying a bird of some sort, from which we may deduce they enjoy this form of exercise. In fact Flat Coats love jumping, which can be taught fairly easily with a low obstacle and the dog on a lead. Giving the command 'over', the handler goes round the side and the dog is encouraged to clear the jump on his own, although occasionally the handler may have to show by example what is required. Once the penny drops and the dog knows what you want he will freely clear all sorts of obstacles which can prove very useful if he is in a postion where the only way out of a field, for example, is by way of a style. Another method of teaching a dog to jump is to use an obstacle in a narrow passage way.

In the old days most gundog training or 'breaking' was in the hands of the gamekeepers, but fortunately, as that old term has lapsed into disuse, so too has the balance of training changed to a woman's perogative, although competitions see about an equal number of both as competitors. As far as Flat Coats go they are still dual purpose dogs and it would be a great pity if they ever lost their working ability and became beautiful but useless. However, there are many people whose interest in the working side is very strong, so at the moment the future looks fairly satisfactory.

8

Showing Your Flat Coat

If you were to ask the man in the street what he knows about dog shows, you would probably gather that he has heard of Crufts, the only championship show to be held in London (taking place each February), but precious few others. There are in fact literally thousands of shows held every year, at venues as far apart as Lands End to John O'Groats. Exhibitors from all over the country attend them, often starting very early in the morning to arrive in time for judging, which usually commences at nine or ten o'clock – at least that is better than on the Continent, for there judging often begins as early as eight o'clock.

Dog shows for those committed to them are more like a way of life. In this country shows are mostly for pedigree dogs (except at exemption level) and all are under the jurisdiction of the Kennel Club, who lay down the rules and regulations that govern the functioning of the four thousand odd gatherings that schedule hundreds of classes for the exhibitors who attend them. I don't think people can remain neutral about dog shows – you either like them or hate them, there seems to be no in between. There is certainly a large turn over of people who start off in the sport and then fall by the wayside, but there are also a hard core of exhibitors who turn up religiously, win or lose, because it is their hobby. There is no closed season but most of the top shows or 'Championship' ones (where basically you can make up a champion if you have the dog and the luck plus the know how) are held outdoors from April to September, but it would be possible to exhibit somewhere every week throughout the year, Saturday and Sunday included, if you and your dog had the stamina required. How does all this start? Well there are as many ways as days in the week, but probably the most common method is that someone buys a dog as a pet, someone else admires it and says 'Why don't you show it?' and so the owner takes the plunge. Everyone starts off as novices because here experience is the teacher. If your dog does well despite your poor handling you are fairly certain to be bitten by the show bug, the symptoms of which manifest themselves in a form of madness consisting of rushing up and down motorways at impossible hours of the morning to get to

Midland Counties Championship Show, Stafford 1984.
(Photograph: John Hartley)

inaccessible show grounds, often in appalling weather.

Dog showing is where my main interest lies and as I have been at the game for well over twenty years I think I may claim to have stayed the course. Like every game there are written and unwritten laws, plus many tips and wrinkles, so for those who have just got their first Flat Coat and someone suggests that it is shown I will attempt to cover something of the general aspects that a novice should know.

This hobby, apart from being time consuming, is also one for those who don't mind being beaten. You can be top of the line one week and bottom the next with the same dog and you have to lose gracefully, for if you can't you are better not exhibiting at all.

People often remark on how well I must be doing financially with all the winning we do, but believe me, I end up at the end of the year literally hundreds of pounds out of pocket. That is not so surprising when you realise that often there is no money at all given as prizes nowadays at a great many of the big shows, and even if there is it is only about £2, £1 and 50p for the first three places. So why do people bother? Really there is no answer to that except that it is like belonging to a select club, the members of which you meet on a regular basis. If you do well that is fine, the glory lasting for that show, but at the end it is past history and there is always the next one to anticipate.

A dog can be shown from the age of six months but he must be registered in your name at the Kennel Club, that is, transferred from the breeder's ownership to yourself. The correct name of the dog on the entry form is obligatory also, and once named cannot be changed except by the addition of the new owner's affix (or kennel name). If the dog has not been named by the breeder this must be put right as soon as possible and then the entry form can be completed with the initials NAF added to it ('Name Applied For'). This leaves the way open for a change of name should the Kennel Club decide your choice is unacceptable. Another abbreviation seen in catalogues from time to time is TAF which means 'Transfer Applied For'.

Entry forms can be obtained from the secretary of the society holding the show. When you are an established show-goer you will probably receive a schedule (by the way the English way of pronouncing this is 'shed-' not the Americanised 'sked-') through the post because you showed at the same show last time. Other methods of finding out about shows is through the local paper, the dog press *Dog World* and *Our Dogs*, or a poster in the pet shop window. Whatever the source of the information the type of show being held must be stated. There are seven types, starting from the least important, the exemption, to the top which is a championship one.

All require permission from the Kennel Club but only Limited, Open and Championship shows require licences. Just to explain the differences, the Exemption Show is the one usually run in conjunction with the village fete, local gymkhana, flower show or similar function. It is divided into two sections, the first one has four classes – usually Puppy, Sporting, Non Sporting and Open – and is for pedigree dogs, although they do not have to be registered at the Kennel Club, and from which the 'Best in Show' is chosen; the second part is of eight classes and anyone can enter classes such as the 'Dog with the Waggiest Tail', Fancy Dress etcetera. Dogs that have won a Challenge Certificate are not eligible.

Show type number two is a Match which can be a competition between a single breed or a number of breeds not exceeding sixty-four dogs in all, run by a registered society or club and is a good place to initiate a youngster into ring behaviour. Again, any dog who has won a Challenge Certificate is not allowed to compete. What happens is that members pay a small sum, twenty or thirty pence for example, and receive a number. These are put in a hat and

A typical show pose. (Photograph: David Dalton)

drawn out in pairs and these two dogs compete against each other, so you could have an Irish Wolfhound and a tiny Chihuahua against each other. The winner of each pair goes forward to the next round until eventually there are two left for Best in Match and Reserve.

A Primary Show can only schedule eight classes, the highest of which is maiden (for dogs not having won a first prize in any show except as a puppy) and is not often offered by societies as it is rather restricted. They may not start before 2 p.m. at a weekend.

Sanction Shows on the other hand, may begin at 12.30 p.m. and can offer ten classes for one breed or twenty-five classes for more than one breed up to Post Graduate, and limits a dog's previous wins to five firsts at Championship shows at Post Graduate or above, so again Challenge Certificate winners are exempt. In contrast to the previous types of shows, Sanction events must produce a schedule giving the name of the judge.

The fifth classification is a 'Limited' show which is only open to certain people, usually the members of a particular canine club or society, although if you don't already belong it is usually only a matter of paying the subscription. This type of show and the two higher ones require licences from the Kennel Club and not just permission. There are usually between twenty-one and fifty classes if more than one breed is scheduled. Challenge Certificate winners are not allowed to compete and judges must be notified in the schedule.

Open Shows are, as the name implies, for all dogs for which breed classes are scheduled, so Champions and Challenge Certificate winners may take part. Exhibitors do not have to be members of the Society holding the show, although there are often inducements like cheaper entry fees if you do. Usually held on one day they do sometimes stretch to two.

At the top of the list is the Championship Show which may be held by a single society for one particular breed, for example the Flat Coated Retriever Society, or a general society such as West of England Ladies, Bath or Birmingham, when classes are held for most of the recognised breeds. There are however one or two specialised group championship shows such as the United Retriever Club or National Gundog for our breed, while other groups have similar events.

In 1987 there were twenty-five general shows offering Challenge Certificates for Flat Coats plus three individual societies (Gundog Breeds of Scotland, Gundog Society of Wales and Merseyside Gundog) in addition to two National Gundog Shows, one held by the United Retriever Club and the other by the Flat Coat Breed Championship, making a total of thirty-two at which a champion may be made up. In 1986 (the latest figures at the time of writing) there were 529 Championship Shows licensed that were held on any of the seven days of the week, the most famous being Crufts. It is the only Championship Show that is held in London and starts the round of top shows off again in February for another year, although as I've already pointed out, the other six types of shows go on all the time. It took place at Olympia for over thirty years and prior to that at the Royal Agricultural Hall in Islington, where it began in 1891 under the direction of the founder Charles Cruft, from whom it takes its name. 1978 was the last time the show was held at Olympia, after which it moved to Earls Court, increasing from a two day to a four day event with world wide coverage. In view of the time of year many people would prefer a summer event out in the country but I doubt if that will ever happen.

The top award at Championship Shows are called Challenge Certificates and go to the best dog and best bitch on the day in the judge's opinion and the Best of Breed comes from one of these two. All the Best of Breeds go forward to compete in their groups of which there are six – Toy, Terrior, Utility, Hound, Working and Gundog – and these six winners are then in the final line up from which the Best in Show is chosen. A dog (or bitch) winning three Challenge Certificates under three different judges in the gundog group is entitled to put the letters 'Sh Ch' or Show Champion in front of their name (subject to the Kennel Club approval), they then have to qualify in the field in order to gain their full title and drop the 'Sh', although other groups can become full Champions straight away.

These then are the seven types of shows and as I have already explained those licensed as Limited, Open or Championship events need schedules plus entry forms which are enclosed with them. I would advise you to try and enter at one of the two lower levels rather than plunge in at the deep end of a Championship show without any prior experience, for your own benefit as much as anything. You will need to obtain a schedule and the relevant entry form, although at a pinch they are all printed to the same format so basically any dog show entry form would do. Do read the schedule through carefully so that the entry form is filled in correctly, for mistakes are costly in time, money and temper to rectify, especially if the secretary has to phone you up to correct them. If slips as to dogs' names or breeding occur then, when they are discovered, the dog runs the risk of being disqualified from any awards by the Kennel Club. This happened to me for I entered a young dog in his sister's name instead of his own, don't ask me why, and as luck would have it he won two classes that day at a Championship Show. Both awards were withdrawn by the Kennel Club when I realised what had happened and wrote to acquaint them with the facts.

The closing date for the receipt of entries will be on the schedule and is usually given as a certain date of posting, with a few days leeway to allow for holdups in the post. After this date has passed any further entries received are usually returned to the sender. Most show entry forms are produced either by Highams Press from Derby, who have done it for years, or more recently by a form called Fosse Data which is computer based, but the basic layout is very similar. The dog's registered name comes in the first column and then the column for NAF and TAF, which I explained earlier was 'Name or Transfer Applied For', after which comes the columns for the breed, followed by sex, date of birth, breeder, sire and dam. If the breeder is yourself it is permissable to write 'owner' in that column, otherwise it should be the name of the owner of the bitch at the time of whelping. On the old type of form, following the columns for sire and dam, there used to be one for price which you filled in if you wished to sell the dog, and once having filled in that column you were bound to sell to anyone offering that amount of money, even if in the interim you had changed your mind.

The final column on the form is for you to write the numbers of the classes you wish to enter. This can sometimes cause a problem

A completed Application Form

MANCHESTER DOG SHOW SOCIETY

CHAMPIONSHIP SHOW

Will be held under Kennel Club Rules and Show Regulations

The Exhibition Halls, Belle Vue, Manchester

Thursday 19th March 1987 — Working
Friday 20th March 1987 — Utility & Toys
Saturday 21st March 1987 — Gundogs
Sunday 22nd March 1987 — Hounds & Terriers

MANCHESTER
DOG SHOW SOCIETY
FOUNDED
1861

Entries Close: TUESDAY 3rd FEBRUARY 1987

ENTRY FEES FOR EACH DOG ENTERED

First Entries (Breeds with CCs) @ £1.50	£
First Entries (Breeds without CCs) @ £4.00	£
Not for Competition @ £2.50	£
Subsequent Entries (except Stakes) @ 50p	£
Stakes Entries @ £4.00	£
Puppy Lincoln @ £2.50	£
KCJO Stakes @ £1.00	£
Car Park @ £1.00	£

Enclosed Cheque Postal Order £ ....
Payable to Manchester Dog Show Society
BENCHING FREE   All Fees include VAT

MANCHESTER DOG SHOW SOCIETY entries are processed by FOSSE DATA SYSTEMS
You may enter ALL your breeds on one entry form

This form must be used by one person only (or partnership)

Writing MUST BE IN INK OR INDELIBLE PENCIL

REGISTERED NAME OF DOG (and NAF if Name applied for and TAF if Transfer applied for)	BREED	Sex D or B	Full Date of Birth	BREEDER (if owner put owner)	SIRE (BLOCK LETTERS)	DAM (BLOCK LETTERS)	To be entered in Classes numbered
RASE GLADIATOR	FLAT COAT RETRIEVER	D	16.12.83	OWNER	WOODLAND WHIPCORD	RASE LAPWING	110

(Please use block capitals)

NAME OF OWNER(S) MRS P M PETCH
(Mr Mrs Miss)
ADDRESS GREENACHES GALLAMORE LANE
MIDDLE RASEN MARKET RASEN LINCS
POSTCODE LN8 3HZ TEL (STD)

Entries and Fees which MUST BE PREPAID to be sent to:
The Secretary: R T KEENAN, The Hollies, 279 Rake Lane, Clifton Junction, Swinton, Manchester M27 2LL. Tel: 061 794 2678

DECLARATION

I undertake to abide by the Rules and Regulations of The Kennel Club and of this Show and I declare that the dogs entered have not suffered from or been knowingly exposed to any infectious or contagious disease during the six weeks prior to exhibition and I will not exhibit them if they incur such risks between now and the day of the Show. I declare that to the best of my knowledge the dogs are not liable to disqualification under Kennel Club Show Regulations.

Usual Signature of Owner(s) P M Petch   Date 6.2.87

Note: Dogs entered in breach of Kennel Club Show Regulations are liable to disqualification whether or not the owner was aware of the breach.   KENNEL CLUB

FOSSE DATA SYSTEMS LTD. Street Ashton. Rugby CV23 0PL Tel: Rugby (0788) 833132

80

because once the dog is out of junior class at the age of eighteen months, entry to the later classes is governed by what the dog has previously won; sometimes it is simpler to enter a high class like Limit rather than the one before it, Post Graduate, if the latter is likely to be very large in numbers. As one has no idea of the opposition likely to be encountered until one actually arrives at a show this can pose a problem.

The class definitions are set out in each schedule along with all other relevant information. With a young dog it is better to limit the number of classes entered to two or at most three, especially if, as in Limited and Open Shows, these classes could be spread out in the schedule. A youngster gets tired and easily bored standing around a ring waiting for large entries in classes to be judged. Therefore with a young dog you are probably better just entering the breed classes, which at least come altogether, after which it is often possible to leave the show and wait to add the varieties until the dog is older. With a youngster AV (Any Variety) Retriever Novice is allowable, but I should wait to go into AV Retriever Open until later on in the dog's career. The competition in these classes is quite strong as they are open for all five Retriever breeds (the sixth one, Nova Scotia Duck Tolling Retrievers, are not yet registered in this country, although I have seen these dogs abroad). An Open class of any sort means that it is able to be entered by any aged dog, but entry is not obligatory. One important rule is that once your dog is over twelve months and out of puppyhood he must be entered in a breed class, if one is scheduled, before being able to enter in the variety classes, the only exception to this being Veterans and dogs entered on an AV Field Trial Class. For some time up to September 1986 Champions entered in the Special Champion Stakes sponsored by Pedigree Chum were also exempt from breed entry, but that has now been rescinded and they too must enter breed classes first.

One tip to remember is that if you are entering more than one dog it is worth putting a note on the outside of the schedule as to whom you have entered in what. At the bottom of the entry form there is a paragraph that is headed Declaration that requires the exhibitor's signature to the fact that the dog has not been in contact with or actually suffered from any infections or contageous disease during the previous six weeks. This is followed by the statement that to the best of the exhibitor's knowledge the dog is not liable to disqualification under Kennel Club show regulations. Although not actually stated, the show regulations referred to cover disabilities such as not being blind or deaf, not showing a spayed bitch (one with the womb removed) or castrated dog. A dog that is termed a cryptorchid (a male whose testicles have not descended) or a monochid (where one has not descended) is not actually barred from being shown these days, although in earlier days this was the case, but people do not usually bother because both these conditions are very serious faults.

Space on the right of the form is for the name and address of the exhibitor plus at least one other space for a request for next year's schedule, and often another on a resumé for the secretary's benefit. To save time I use printed name and address sticky labels instead of actually writing out my address three times. Before sending off the completed form with a cheque or postal order for the amount outstanding for the entries, do check that you haven't made any silly mistakes, that all the information given is correct and that it is signed properly. Try and post early if possible, for it makes the secretary's job easier if all the forms don't come in a rush at the end, and do use First Class Post so that the form arrives in time for the closing date for entries. It is also a sensible precaution to get a certificate of posting so that if there are any problems over checking entry dates you have the proof that yours was sent in time. Apart from a Championship show when you do receive passes, you do not get any feed back but just turn up on the appointed day, at the specified time for judging. It is often worth giving the secretary a ring during the week preceeding the show (don't leave it till the night before when he or she will be up to their eyes in preparation for the big day) if your judge is scheduled to do several breeds, for you may save yourself an unnecessarily early start or a considerable wait on arrival. Check with the schedule to see if passes are to be sent, and if they are and yours have not been received three or four days before the event ring the secretary to see if she received your entries. If she hasn't this is where your proof of posting can be used to advantage. If your entries have got lost in the post you will have a wasted journey to the show as you will not be in the catalogue and therefore will not be eligible to take part.

If you are placed in your classes you will receive a prize card according to your position: red is first (although in America blue takes top billing), blue second, yellow third and green reserve or fourth. Anything below that, for example Very Highly Commended, Highly Commended, Commended etcetera, can be any colour although white is often used for VHC. Prize money is often, regretably, a thing of the past in Championship shows although Open shows still pay £1, 50p and 25p to the first three place winners, with the money in an envelope stapled to the card. If a Championship show does give prize money it is usually in voucher form attached to the prize card. This is exchanged by the Treasurer after a

*A dual-purpose bitch Ch Torwood Poppet (Heronsflight Tercel ×
Heronsflight Puff) owned by Mrs J. Griffiths.
(Photograph: Roger Chambers)*

certain time, the money awarded being £2, £1 and 50p. Crufts at one
time gave £4, £2 and £1 but even there, no money is now given to
the winners of breed classes, although there is sponsorship of groups
stakes and Best in Show by firms such as Pedigree Chum. A tip
worth remembering is that not everyone is as honest as you and I, so
don't put your prize card up over your bench without first detaching
the counterfoil.

Rosettes are awarded as well as prize cards in some cases – mostly
at Open and Limited Shows, although some Championship Societies
give rosettes for both Challenge Certificate winners. They are in the
same four colours as the cards plus some really pretty ribbons for
Best of Breed, Reserve Best of Breed, Best Opposite Sex, Best
Puppy and so on. Rosettes can make a very colourful wall if you
decide to put them up, provided of course you consistently win at
shows where they are awarded. In addition, at many of the gundog
society shows there are a number of cups and trophies on offer for
Best Gundog, Best of Breed and many other awards in the form of
shields, plaques, rose bowls, tankards or trays. These are usually
held from show to show, which may be annual or twice yearly, and

some shows provide little replicas that the winners can keep permanently, which are nice to have.

Times of judging vary with the type of show but the most usual commencement is at ten a.m. for Flat Coats although the very heavily subscribed breeds like Irish Setters, Golden Retrievers, Afghans, Dobermanns etcetera will often commence judging a full hour earlier, which can mean a very early start from home. Most of the smaller shows start any time from twelve noon to two o'clock and these days times of removal are pretty flexible. Because of pressure of public opinion many societies have relaxed the once rigid rule of early removals not being before three or four o'clock – many people travel long distances and have no help at home so there is a need to get back as soon as possible. Therefore the 'coffee housing' that went on in the old days is now a thing of the past, which is a pity, but it merely mirrors the pace at which most of us live these days. Crufts still has a six p.m. removal, but this is only to be expected from 'Dogdom's Shop Window' – empty benches would not be much of an advertisement. If there is a definite time for removal and you break the rule and slip out through a hole in the fence, you stand the chance of being reported to the Kennel Club and can incur a fine, or in an extreme case even a ban from showing for a stipulated time, but fortunately with the easing of this contentious ruling the temptation to disobey is far less.

The larger shows, where there are over two hundred dogs in the individual breed entries, must provide benching. These benches are three sided partitions which make a frontless cage with the dog's number up over the top. At smaller events people tie their dogs to convenient fixtures or leave them in the car (providing it is not too hot) until time for their class. The dog's number is the one given to each dog for the duration of that show and is listed in the catalogue with the details of owner, breeding, date of birth etcetera, so that interested people can check on any particulars they wish to know. The numbers are sometimes sent with the passes by some Championship Societies, otherwise they are distributed in the ring by the steward or collected off the benches themselves, where the duplicates are laid on the bottom. Smaller shows tend to have them on the secretary's table near the door on entry. There is no hard and fast rule, one just has to wait and see which is the order of the day on arriving at each different show.

At the age of eighteen months a dog leaves behind classes entered according to how old he is, and he can then try for higher things. He is eligible for an award called the Junior Warrant up to this age, which is a funny anomaly as it doesn't really benefit the recipient very much except that is an honour to win the certificate. A dog has to collect twenty-five points to do so – these are awarded on a scale of three per Championship show win and one per Open show in breed classes only. Not many Flat Coats managed to get Junior Warrants in the past because there were very few breed classes scheduled. It is easier now that the breed is growing and more classes are put on at Open shows so that the chances of qualifying are much improved, but it still means that if you wish to add these letters to your dog's name you must be willing to travel all over the country to shows where the breed is scheduled. When you have amassed your points you must fill in the necessary form showing relevent wins and claim from the Kennel Club because no-one will run after you about it.

Winners of Limit and Open classes plus the second and third placed dogs are eligible for the stud book and consequently now also qualify for entry to Crufts. These stud numbers often appear beside the name of the sire and dam on a pedigree form. Other stud book qualifiers are Challenge Certificate winners plus Reserve Challenge Certificate and Field Trial class winners. The stud book qualifiers vary from time to time as the Kennel Club alters the classes eligible, so by the time you read this they may have changed again.

The way in which any dog is presented in the show ring can make or marr his chances of success. A clever handler can disguise the faults of a mediocre animal or make a good one look like a star. A Flat Coat is no different in this respect than any other dog but because he is a whole colour and black at that, he does not appear to be as flashy as the Pointer or English Setter, for example, in the ring. However there are certain points that are worth bearing in mind which help to get round this problem. First, it is very difficult to see the outline of a black dog if the handler is wearing a dark skirt or trousers, so try to wear light coloured clothes, at least on the nether regions. Shoes should be light and sensible so as not to put off other exhibits, and clanking, jangling jewellery or dangling ear-rings do not do much to help show your dog off to advantage either. Second, a nervous dog that is not used to crowds or an audience can often stand as if unsound, as for example cow-hocked or with his toes turned in or spread out, so make sure that your dog is confident by taking him among people before you take him into a ring. The third case in point is that one should never draw attention to a fault in your dog with your hand, by touching the tail or offending part, and when standing the animal turn it so that any blemish is on the side nearest to yourself not the judge. Lastly, always concentrate while you are in the ring by keeping one eye on the judge, whatever 'coffee-housing' you may be doing at the same time.

Swallowflight Black Justin from Holland. Owned by Mrs Goede van Demburg. (Photograph: David Dalton)

There are several unwritten rules about showing, the first of which is that it is not done to show a dog under a judge if they were the breeder. Although the Kennel Club rules state that twelve months must elapse from the date of the change of ownership, it is still something not to be recommended. Another point is that if a judge has already awarded a dog a Challenge Certificate it should not be shown under that judge again, the only exception being at Crufts, which is the canine window on the world. It is also most unfair on any dogs being shown to take a bitch on heat, or in season, to a show because a dog's nose goes down on the ground and it is very difficult to show him to advantage when there is a strong competing scent.

Prior to arriving at a show you need to have your Flat Coat in tip top condition with the shiny coat, bright eyes and cold nose that come with correct feeding and exercise. He should be able to move freely on a loose lead, stand fair and square while the judge examines him, allow his mouth to be opened for his teeth to be looked at, his tail extended and his feet lifted without squirming about or collapsing in a heap, thus making judging a pleasure not a penance. He will have been brushed and combed and made tidy, which means that his ears will have had all the old hair pulled out with a plucking knife to lie flat and neat against the side of the head. Feathering will be profuse but not too long, any extra will also have been removed.

Feet should be round and tight; to get them like this hold the foot in the left hand while the right pulls any spare tufts from between the toes so that they may be cut off – trim from the bottom upwards with the serrated shears that are indispensable for this job. Ordinary scissors finish off the task by cutting round and under the outline of the foot, making the whole paw neat and tidy. The growth of hair on the back legs between the hock and the pastern should be sheared in the same manner so as to lie flat and close – do not use ordinary scissors here for they can leave jagged edges showing the cutting line. The length of tail only needs to cover the last joint, any surplus hair being removed by the plucking knife, but keep the point in the shaped end. A bath leaves a Flattie's coat fluffy and therefore should not be given within three days of the date of the show, and likewise do not let your dog get into water until he has come out of the ring, although sometimes that is easier said than done for this breed loves nothing better than to be as wet as possible.

All major grooming should be completed at home prior to the great day, so that all that is needed at the show is a final spit and polish with brush, comb and a soft chamois leather. All grooming equipment needs to be kept together and I use a leather zip pouch that was originally intended for pens and pencils but does the job admirably. In addition one needs a show bag for articles such as benching chains, kennel name-plate, bowls, dishes, towels etcetera. A show lead is a must and various types are obtainable. I use a rope field trial one, or a long leather one with a ring in the end that serves as both collar and lead together. It is also quite common to use a nylon lead in a colour to suit your particular shade of dog, but they do tend to cut into your hand if the dog pulls in the opposite direction all of a sudden.

At the bigger shows in England, three sided metal cages called benches are provided as a temporary home for the exhibits when not in the ring or being exercised, and Kennel Club regulations lay down that proper collars and chains have to be provided to secure the animal to the bench for this period. Choke chains or ordinary leads are not suitable as dogs have been known to partially hang themselves if they fall off and cannot get back, so they must be tethered short. Ring numbers are worn on the front of the jacket of an exhibitor and special pins bearing the head of the different breeds are now available for this purpose.

Covering for the benches needs to be brought and carpet squares, blanket or various other materials can be purchased from show stands. I also carry a bottle of water as sometimes it can be a time-consuming hike to the nearest tap, plus dishes for both food

Sh Ch Hallbent Kim and Hallbent Serenade. Owned and bred by Georgie Buchanan. (Photograph: David Dalton)

and water, although one would do for both. I usually take milk in addition but biscuit meal and meat (either canned, frozen or in chubs) can be easily obtained at one or other of the many stands vying for trade at these events; you will need a knife or spoon to dish it out providing you have remembered a tin opener, if not many stands will open the tin for you.

The night before a show, particularly if I have a five or six a.m. start (which is never my best time), I collect up passes, schedule, pens, purse and leads plus show bag and put them handy for picking up in the morning, making sure my show number pin is attached to my jacket, so that I don't have to think any more about them except to pick them up as I leave at the usual gallop. Why is it one is always short of time? Of course if you have kind friends in the show vicinity, or go down with the caravan for the weekend, life is very much easier.

On the day of the show try to arrive with time to spare before you are due to go in the ring – no dog is at its best if rushed straight from the car into a class, especially if he has not had time to relieve himself after a long journey. One of the first jobs on arrival at a show is to obtain a catalogue to make sure that no mistakes have occurred and your dog is entered in his correct classes with the correct details of breeding and ownership. If there is a mistake go straight to the secretary and get it put right before you enter the ring otherwise you render your dog liable to be disqualified by the Kennel Club from any awards he may gain.

Be ready for your class when it is called, the only exception to this is if you are in another ring at the same time and then the steward must be informed so that the judge will wait for you to get back. You should wear your ring number on entering the ring – this will usually be obtained from the ring steward as the class is called, but sometimes is to be found on the bench or with the secretary, depending on the size of the show. On entering the ring make sure that the dog is securely held on his show lead so that you are in complete control should any untoward incidents occur. If you use titbits in the ring, and it is better not to if at all possible, do try to make them as unobtrusive as you can for loud rustling noises can distract the dog in front of yours, causing it to turn round at a crucial time such as just as the judge is looking in his direction.

On entering the ring the steward will tell you on which side the judge wishes the unseen dogs to stand and you and the other new dogs form a line. It is not usual to stand in any order but the old hands usually go first. Should this be your first attempt at showing I suggest you get in the middle so that from whichever end the judge begins you will see what others are required to do before it is your turn. When all exhibits are in the ring some judges take a walk along the line of dogs first, before asking anyone to move, and this is where your dog needs to be set up or placed in a standing show pose. Flat Coats are not topped and tailed like Setters, that is, held with head and tail extended, but should stand naturally on a loose lead with feet not splayed out but tight like a cat's, and facing forward with the handler either standing in front of the dog or right behind. The dog must be balanced with his forefeet under the shoulders a little way apart, also making sure that the hindfeet are not too far back as to make the dog look overstretched. One of the Flat Coat's most attractive points is the gaily waving plumed tail which should be carried level with the back both when the dog is standing and when it is on the move – a gay tail is a fault.

If there is room to do so, many judges then commence by asking exhibits to run round the ring so that they can obtain an overall picture of each dog's movement. If this is the case keep your dog on the left of you (for usually everyone moves to the right) which is the side nearest to the judge, for it is worth remembering that it is the dogs' movement he is interested in, not the handlers'. Move in

Indian file, making sure your dog keeps a distance from the dog in front and behind and do not crowd but use all the space at your disposal. Each dog is examined individually in rotation and when it is your turn once you have set up your Flat Coat do not overhandle; while the judge is going over him stand to the side, loosen the lead and keep out of the way while the front is being looked at, moving round to hold the head while the rest of the dog comes under scrutiny. You may not make conversation with the judge but must, of course, answer any questions that you are asked, for example the dog's age. Having completed the examination of the dog, the judge may ask you to move in a triangle or straight up and down the ring once or even twice. When you have finished that manoeuvre (and do make sure if you are asked for a triangle you put in three distinct corners) join the line of seen dogs, next to the dog you were behind in the original formation. It is now possible to relax a little and even chat to your fellow exhibitors, but keep a weather eye on the judge, for you may get no warning from the steward that all dogs have been seen and that your dog needs setting up again for the final selection. Some judges pull out their finalists in the order they will eventually place them, while others pull out several on a short list for the first four places and then make their choice in order of merit after moving them all again, so remember you have not won until you have the red card in your hand, and go on showing your dog until you get it. If you are in the group left out of the short list the steward will probably say something like 'Finished with the rest'. Leave the ring thinking to yourself that there is always the next show and never grumble, either about the judge or his finalists, for we all have our good days and our bad, and if you cannot take a beating in this game I suggest you give up dog showing and find another hobby that is less competitive.

If the judge says 'I'm not placing you' or 'I've not finished', this is a warning that he has not finally made up his mind about placings so you must be aware of what is happening. The steward's job is to hand out the prize cards and take a note of the placings for the records, so do stand still for this to happen, also the judge will probably need to write a critique on the first two dogs placed, in order to write his results up for the dog papers.

If you are entered for the next class join the 'seen' dogs, placing yourself in the order in which you were pulled out in the last class, then when the new ones have been judged the dogs from the former class join the line to be considered along with them for the next set of awards. It is usual to congratulate the winner of the class if you find yourself further down the line.

A dog or bitch unbeaten by any other of the same sex is entitled to compete at a Championship Show for the Challenge Certificate (three of which makes up a Champion) the two winners then vie for the Best of Breed award. At an Open Show scheduling breed classes, winners of the classes, whatever their sex, are entitled to compete for Best of Breed; where there are no breed classes any unbeaten dog can go straight through for Best in Show, but this is usually at a small show.

Best of Breeds at the Championship Shows go forward into the groups so the Best Flat Coat will compete in the gundog group (there are six of these altogether) and each of the six group winners will go into the Best in Show ring at the end, when the best dog and reserve are chosen by the judge for the day. Remember to only wear the Best of Breed rosette when competing in the group and not in any of the variety classes when it must be removed before entering the ring.

It is a good idea to check the list of cups and trophies if you have had a successful day to see if your dog is eligible for any of them. Don't do what I did when a very green novice and disappear after winning a class, thus losing a chance of competing for Best of Breed; stay around until after judging is finished.

If you are a novice exhibitor there is a lot to learn and this can best

Pauline Westrops three champions Halstock Primula of Ravenscrest, Falswift Auriga and Falswift Apperition. (Photograph: David Dalton)

Mrs C. Dugdale's Ch and Can Am Ch Parkburn Dextensing of Casuarina winning his English title at the SKC May 1978 under Mr Walter Bradshaw

be done by keeping eyes and ears open and asking questions of the old hands at the game. Most Flat Coat people are only too willing to help the newcomer get on the right road. Often the judge when he has finished in the ring will explain his point of view on the interpretation of the Standard. It is worth remembering, however, that a judge sees on the day what he has in front of him and therefore it is better not to seek the reason why you may have been unsuccessful on this occasion. It is all a matter of opinion, and next week the order could well be reversed.

If you do win Best of Breed and you can possibly remain till the group judging at the end of the show, it is good manners and courtesy to your judge to do so, otherwise the breed remains unrepresented in the final line up.

If you learn to lose with a good grace and win without crowing about it, you are likely to get the most out of this time-consuming hobby.

9

Health and Fitness

The Flat Coat on the whole is a fairly hardy breed for a pedigree dog, no more liable to catch anything than any other canine. One of the reasons some people give for preferring a mongrel is that they are not subject to so many illnesses. However in my experience cross breeds can be carriers, even if not actually themselves suffering from viruses like kennel cough, especially if they are allowed to roam the streets at will. One modern day scourge which is no respecter of pedigrees and affects all breeds alike (although it is easier to keep a check where numbers of a breed are registered) to say nothing of human deaths from it, is of course cancer. Looking at the cause of Flat Coats being put down I believe that this disease is responsible for the highest number of premature deaths in the breed.

One might expect Flat Coats to be able to stand up to all types of weather conditions when one thinks of their ancestry and realises that the Newfoundland coasts have very severe winters, but they do need plenty of warmth as babies in the nest. I remember losing some of my very first litter, born in the winter, because I did not realise that they required a heat lamp. Since then I have usually managed to rear summer litters without heat but find that those born in the winter do need the extra comfort of a lamp, although now of course, with the introduction of Vet-Bed and similar products it is not as imperative as it was when I started breeding twenty odd years ago.

The thick coats of the Flatties help protect them when working in heavy cover or undergrowth and also if involved in a fight (which fortunately is not often as they are not quarrelsome dogs) but accidents can happen. Some people keep a special medical chest for their dogs but if you do not, you must be able to lay hands on articles like the Dettol bottle, cotton wool, scissors, etcetera, pretty quickly should the need arise. An antiseptic puffer of sulphanilamide is also indispensible, plus other aids like a tube of eye ointment, powder for ear canker, liquid paraffin, a bottle of veterinary shampoo, pills for both round and tape worms, a flea spray and a thermometer which are needed from time to time. A number of these articles can be bought locally but I do tend to get my requirements from my vet as I find that although there are many proprietory brands on the market, it is easy to waste money trying first one and then another before finding a cure that works for your dog's problem. If you do find it necessary to consult your veterinary surgeon about a persistent problem of health or hygiene do go sooner rather than later, and spare a thought for the poor soul for they get precious little time with their families, so don't wait until Sunday night to ring him with a problem that could be dealt with quite easily during the day. Having said that, I am sure that your vet would rather be called too soon than the other way round, for any ailment or disease caught early responds to treatment much more easily than one left till later.

A healthy dog means a happy dog and both these conditions can occur providing the dog is correctly fed and given sufficient love, training and exercise, but the most important of these is the feeding, for it is this that produces the loose supple skin and shiny coat, free from sores, scurf and dust. One should be able to pick up a handful of skin and feel the muscles ripple underneath. No dog should have offensive breath for the gums and teeth should be firm and white, set in a clean mouth. Eyes should be clear and bright and there should be no mattery discharge. The ears should also be clean and dry with no canker which can take either the wet form, which causes the ear to crackle, or a thick brown gunge, both of which conditions are painful and cause the animal discomfort. The rectum should not be inflamed nor should there be any discharge from the penis.

It does no harm to a dog to go without food now and again. In fact, Denes the canine herbalists recommend one fasting day a week in their scheme of feeding. A dog vomits fairly readily so do not worry unduly if yours is sick occasionally, for they often eat grass for this reason. However do watch to see that nothing more serious is being developed, often coupled with listlessness, lack of energy and appetite, for catching the trouble early may prevent more serious problems later, as I have already mentioned.

Before I go on to look at various conditions, which for ease of referral I have listed alphabetically, I will mention one or two ordinary things like cuts and bleeding. Cuts are fairly common and as long as they are not too deep they can be dealt with easily by the owner. First they need washing in warm water and Dettol to clean them, then sulphanilamide powder puffed into the wound. The dog's licking seems to help the healing process too. For a badly cut place, cover with lint and cotton wool, wrap round with a bandage or adhesive tape and take the patient to the vet for stitches as soon as possible. Should an artery have been severed, when blood will be pumping out, put a tight bandage (a handkerchief would do in an

Maybrian Trail Blazer, owned and bred by Mr and Mrs B. Pash.

emergency) on the nearest pressure point above the cut, then use a pen or pencil to tighten the tourniquet to stop the bleeding. Remember that it will need loosening at least once every ten minutes so that the leg or whatever is not deprived of blood altogether. Again, seek veterinary assistance as soon as possible.

I understand that dogs can suffer from the common cold symptoms, although I have never had one that has, but the treatment is similar to that of humans.

One other tip: it is worth noting if the dog continually brushes his mouth with his paw or shakes his head, check to see if there is a piece of bone or a stick jammed across the roof of the mouth or between the teeth.

ABSCESSES   Inflammation caused by pus under the skin, usually very red and painful and can occur almost anywhere. The swelling usually increases very quickly until it bursts, discharging pus and blood. It can be as a result of a bite or grass seeds and the treatment is often to use a hot Kaolin poultice (not too hot) to bring it to a head and then bathe in Dettol or salt and hot water. If it shows no sign of bursting it is best to get the vet's advice as it may need lancing and treatment with antibiotics.

ADMINISTERING MEDICINES   This can be done quite simply and without fuss if you sit the dog against a wall, so that he cannot back away, and tip medicine down a pouch of loose skin taken from the side of the mouth, stroking the throat to cause him to swallow. If the medicine is in pill or powder form put your finger in the corner of the mouth behind the teeth and hold it open with your hand. Meanwhile, throw pills as far back as you can. If you practice you can tip them right to the back of the throat. Powders are a bit more difficult but the same rules apply. Then message the throat so that the dog swallows because I have known them hold pills for ages and then spit them out.

ANAEMIA   This is a blood condition showing symptoms of poor health. The gums and eye membranes are very pale and the dog has little appetite or energy, becoming tired very quickly. Often the breathing is laboured and abnormally quick. Iron tablets should be given to combat this condition. Liver, either raw or cooked, is another source of iron and should be fed several times a week.

ANAL GLAND   These scent glands are found in both dogs and bitches each side of the tail or anus. They are pear-shaped sacs containing a dirty deep brown secretion which smells foul and is usually discharged through tiny pores daily. If the dog's motions are too loose then these openings become blocked, which causes inflammation and swelling of the glands. Dogs suffering from this painful complaint draw themselves along the ground in a sitting position and will lick or bite continuously at the tail. This condition is similar to that of worms and that should be looked to first before treatment is effected. It is possible for the Flat Coat owner to learn how to squeeze out the anal glands but he needs to be shown properly by a vet, as these glands are very deep-seated and unless pressure is applied in the right place great pain can be caused. Trouble with the anal glands can result in wet eczema around the base of the tail which must be dried off with powder (*see* eczema, p. 102).

BAD BREATH Known in veterinary circles as halitosis, this can arise from several causes but in nearly all cases it is bad teeth at fault. Gastric troubles often due to worms or kidney failure can be the cause in older dogs, though in the latter cases there are generally other warning symptoms as well. Have the dog's teeth examined by the vet and any decayed ones removed. Amplex tablets help to remove odours, especially if the bad breath is due to eating unsavoury food. If the cause is not in the teeth consult your vet as to further treatment.

BITES Luckily Flat Coats do not often fight with other dogs and unless you are unlucky enough to have a case of kennel jealousy you will probably not be faced with dog bites at all. Occasionally a rat can inflict a nasty wound which can lead to an abscess, so you need to clip away the coat from the affected place and bathe with Dettol, salt, or other antiseptic. Then I puff in sulphanilamide powder and leave open to the air. A bite that has turned septic may need antibiotic treatment which may mean a visit to the vet. If you are out on moorland and your dog is bitten by a snake, keep him warm and get him quickly to a vet.

BLADDER INFLAMMATION (CYSTITIS) This can be caused in several ways; often if a clean animal cannot get out to relieve himself the bladder becomes distended so that at last he is unable to empty it, causing inflammation; a cold could be another cause, as also stones formed in the bladder or kidneys (they can vary in size from a pea to a nut and are formed from mineral salts deposits). The condition occurs more often in bitches than in dogs and is noticeable when the dog strains to pass water and can only get rid of a few drops at a time; often these are bloodstained accompanied by a strong smell of ammonia. There is obvious pain and discomfort and the vet's advice should be sought, as often an operation is necessary. This condition has a tendency to recur.

BOWEL INFLAMMATION   This can be caused by the cold, but often sharp bones of poultry or rabbit are the culprit. Young puppies may suffer from this as the result of worm infestation or another cause is bacterial infection, but the symptoms are usually the same whatever the cause, with a distended painful abdomen and a great thirst. The dog may be affected by either constipation or diarrhoea and again veterinary advice should be sought.

BURNS AND SCALDS   The most common method of burning is from sitting too near to the fire, be it open or electric, though the latter is the worst offender. It is sometimes possible to drag the dog away before the skin gets affected because the smell of the coat burning gives a warning. If not, bathe the affected part in cold water; really soak it and then you should be able to see how much of the skin is actually burnt. Sometimes it takes a day or two before the blisters appear and break out into a nasty open wound, which can then have antiseptic powder puffed in. With both burns and scalds shock is often a resulting factor so the dog needs to be kept warm and your vet contacted. With regard to scalds these can also cause nasty places as a dog's coat tends to hold the heat. They can be caused by the upsetting of boiling water and they can be serious.

CANKER (OTITIS)   Flat Coats can suffer badly from canker which is the old-fashioned blanket name for ear troubles in dogs. It can come in three forms which are Wet, Dry and Parasitic (or mites) but the condition can also be caused if a grass seed or similar foreign body gets into the ear canal. The usual symptoms are scratching the ear or shaking the head and inside the ear feels warm to the touch. With wet canker you can often hear a crackling sound and I clean the ears out gently with a cotton wool wedge (those made for babies are ideal) and apply a little powder we have made up at the chemist, the recipe for which I now give you. It is a very old one and for a time the iodoform was difficult to obtain but I got my last lot made up at Boots so it is on the general market again:

> 1 part iodoform – 110 grams
> 2 parts zinc oxide – 110 grams
> 8 parts boracic powder *or* boric acid crystals – 110 grams

Pull the ear open to its full depth and drop a dollop of the powder as far down as possible from a small spoon, then pull the flap over the ear opening and gently massage the base of the ear to spread the iodoform fumes. The dogs love this as it gets to the places they cannot reach, and that sounds like the advert for a certain German lager!

Dry Canker has no discharge but the ear appears hot and causes irritation. The powder is the best cure I know for this.

Canker caused by parasites such as lice or ear mites produces a red brown waxy discharge. They are just visible to the naked eye as tiny grey dots and need killing before bacterial infection takes place. Often to be found on cats they can be passed on to dogs in the same house and this is one of the primary sources of dog infection. Again, use the canker powder as before, but make sure to hold the ear flap of one ear down for some time before going on to the other so that the iodoform has a chance to kill the parasites.

As Flat Coats are so fond of the water do make sure that the ears are dry after swimming as wet ears are another cause of infection in this direction.

CHOKING This condition can be caused if the dog plays with an object like a small ball which can be swallowed and sticks in the gullet, but very often it is a piece of bone or large piece of meat that is the culprit, and it has been known for death by asphyxia to result. It is sometimes possible to remove the object with your fingers or a pair of forceps but if it cannot be seen, and you suspect that an obstruction is the cause, get the dog to the vet as soon as possible as the animal could die of suffocation.

COAT All dogs change their coats in the spring and many others in the autumn too. Bitches certainly have two changes of coat and this is quite natural. With proper feeding the coat should be thick and bright. Black can shine beautifully, which is one of the reasons I prefer a black to a liver Flat Coat. A loose coat at times other than those mentioned above is a sign of a blood disorder of some sort and the dog needs to have sulphur or some of the herbal tablets produced for this purpose. Do not bath the dog too often as it takes the oil from his coat but there are times, such as a glorious roll in fox droppings or cow muck, when there is no alternative. In these cases we use a veterinary shampoo such as produced by the Vetzyme people. Once or twice during the Show Season when coats are looking dull we will also bath them, choosing a nice day and shampooing on the lawn and rinsing off with the hose. We find that lifting big dogs in and out of the bath is a damp procedure to say the least.

CONSTIPATION   Another sign of a dog being out of condition is constipation which should be speedily dealt with before a stoppage of the bowels result. It may be due to the fact that the diet is wrong or the dog is having insufficient exercise. The latter should be self-explanatory and very often brown bread plus green vegetables added to the food have the desired effect in the former. If not, a dose of liquid paraffin is as good as anything, although of course you can buy prepared laxatives from all the well-known animal firms.

CYSTS   There are various forms of cysts which are swellings containing a sort of fluid secretion and include sebaceous or skin cysts (very often found on the skin, particularly of old dogs), ovarian cysts (which usually require surgical treatment in the affected bitches) and the most usual form of trouble, that of inter-digital (between the toes) cysts. All these swellings are very often painless unless they become infected when they can cause abscesses. The treatment for cysts is to bathe them until they burst and then try to harden the feet, if they are inter-digital. It is possible, if your dog suffers from sore feet, to buy a wax preparation which forms a protective skin, and some people use Friars Balsam which has the same effect. However, this is very sticky and can cause problems with the coat if allowed to drop on it. The appearance of these cysts usually means the dog is somewhat out of sorts and extra vitamin supplement is needed such as Canoval or Vetzyme.

DEPRAVED APPETITE   This is a condition where the dog eats dirt or faeces of either its own or those of other dogs. I do not include horse droppings because there seems to be some ingredient in fresh manure that has an irresistible call to Flat Coats, at least to ours. This habit must be cured and usually if you can find the cause it will sort itself out. Very often bad worm infestation is the trouble or sometimes it is due to deficiency in the diet of some particular vitamin. The dog must be prevented from making dirt-eating a habit and owners must be very quick to get him away before he has a chance to pick up his droppings, or put him on a lead where other dogs have been defecating. At home it is possible to put pepper over the excretion to discourage him. The treatment is to treat for worms (see p. 109) and also to feed Vetzyme or Canovel tablets, although you can also obtain some herbal pills from a firm such as Denes which fulfil the same purpose.

DIARRHOEA This condition occurs as a result of a number of factors. It could be due to a change of feed or totally unsuitable food, while in puppies it can be due to worms, dirty feeding dishes, or a food too high in protein content, although a cold or chill may also bring it on. The treatment depends on the cause and if due to diet this is easily changed and a start made by starving the animal for twenty-four hours and then putting him on a light diet, also cornflour or water in which rice has been boiled can be added to the food. If there is no improvement take the dog to the vet because continuous diarrhoea is very weakening and indicates a more serious condition.

DISTEMPER This is a group of virus diseases which are often fatal and, even if not, leave behind nervous after-effects like Chorea (St Vitus Dance) or paralysis. However, it is unnecessary for dogs to suffer from distemper as they can be vaccinated against it these days with almost 100 per cent record of success. The symptoms of this disease can be easily missed in the early stages as they are very varied, but usually the dog goes off his food, the eyes become inflamed and there is normally a discharge both from eyes and nose. The temperature will be above normal and the dog will sneeze and cough while often there is persistent diarrhoea. This condition is very contagious and can easily be passed on to other dogs so get the vet to come out to the car and do not even allow your dog on the road, as the infection can be relayed without even coming in contact with the dog that has it. Puppies can be vaccinated from around a few weeks old and again a fortnight later, with very often a third injection if the first has been done before the age of twelve weeks. Three or four days should be allowed after that before taking him amongst other dogs or even where they have been in the street or park, for example.

If you are unfortunate and your dog contracts the disease it is a long business, with the dog needing skilful nursing during his convalescence, because relapses can occur and are very dangerous as the Flat Coat will be very weak and therefore more vulnerable. A light nourishing diet is a must and the dog will have to be encouraged to eat as if he cannot smell he will probably have no interest in food. The eyes will need regular bathing and the nose cleaning out with damp cotton wool and all these dressings must be burnt afterwards. It is worth persevering if the dog is just left weak, but if also suffering from a nervous disorder it is better put down. The moral is to get him vaccinated in the first place.

ECZEMA This is an inflamed condition of the skin causing great irritation. It is often difficult to see the reason for this infected skin condition. It could be due to a certain type of flea to which your dog is allergic or it is thought that these skin irritations can be caused by allergies, but finding out to what substance the dog is sensitive is very difficult and has to be tried by a process of elimination. In hot weather it can also be due to the increase in temperature or to the blood becoming over-heated. The difference between eczema and mange is that the latter is highly contagious. Eczema usually occurs when there is a change of coat in the spring and autumn and I have found that older Flat Coats often become affected. Treatment usually means clipping away the hair and bathing the affected parts with a lotion from the vet. If possible, try to prevent the dog from scratching, even if it means putting a plastic bucket on as a collar.

ENTROPION This is a congenital condition that affects some dogs and I have known Flat Coats to suffer from it. Either the top or bottom eyelid, or both, turn in, rubbing the eye lashes on the eyeball, which causes irritation and weeping. The vet will advise on an operation to cure the trouble. Dogs with this condition should not be used for breeding.

EYE CONDITIONS Many dogs suffer from eye conditions because they sit and gaze into the fire or travel with their heads out of the car window; sleeping in a draught can also cause trouble. Common eye troubles are irritation, inflammation and conjunctivitis. The latter is often the result of the presence of a foreign body, but eye troubles can be a symptom of a serious disease. The dog's eye has a third eyelid which looks pinky in colour and is found in the corner of the eye, providing extra protection when necessary. For treatment in the first instance I usually use an eye lotion, either human or veterinary, and keep an opthalmic tube to squeeze into the eye. If the painful condition does not clear up quickly see the vet and try to prevent the dog from rubbing his eyes, even if it means putting on a preventative collar.

The condition that excites the most interest these days is what is known as PRA or Progressive Retinal Atrophy. Dr Keith Barnett of the Small Animal Centre travels round the country testing dogs' eyes and is the acclaimed expert in this field. This disease can cause blindness by the progressive destruction of the light sensitive tissue at the back of the eye and is inherited. Preliminary Certificates are issued from eighteen months until a dog is five years old when he may then have a permanent certificate if still clear. Dr Barnett will also test for cataract or loss of transparency of the lens of the eye in the same way and most breeders have their stud dogs and brood bitches checked at about the age of eighteen months for obvious reasons. Luckily, so far, Flat Coated Retrievers, as a breed, have not been affected by this condition, unlike the Labradors who have had a lot of trouble in the past, although I believe they are now getting on top of it.

FALSE PREGNANCY This is a condition where the bitch produces milk and generally acts as if she were expecting a litter, making a nest and lining up toys or other objects even though she has not been mated. It usually occurs six to eight weeks after a season and is due to an imbalance of hormones which can be adjusted by a visit to the vet. Some bitches can also make milk in sympathy for another bitch's litter. I had this happen when the daughter of my Champion bitch Rumaigne, Rase Nutmeg, produced her first litter, for both Grandma and Mum fed them quite happily and the puppies did not seem to mind receiving attention from either bitch.

FIGHTS Flat Coats in the main are among the best-tempered dogs I have ever met, but there are exceptions to the rule, and also if one keeps more than one stud dog one stands the chance of kennel jealousy, particularly when the bitches are in season. The only answer then is to keep the two dogs completely separate. If, however, you are called upon to separate two fighters, the best way is for both owners to each grab their dog by the collar and twist to choke the dog into letting go, lifting their forefeet off the ground. I have found that throwing a bucket of water only soaks you and does not separate the dogs. Some people advocate using a heavy coat over both but I have never tried this method. If you are on your own remove all canine bystanders if at all possible and then wade in with a riding crop. I find it upsets me more than the dogs.

FLEAS The dog flea seems to affect Flat Coats as often as other breeds and summer is usually the worst time for infestation. There are some years that seem to be worse than others when there seems to be a regular plague of them. It is important to keep the dog free from fleas as it is host to the tapeworm and anyway I hate to see them scratching themselves. A flea can be various colours from red to black and is about one sixteenth of an inch in size. They can move very quickly and contrary to the usual idea prefer to run rather than jump. They are difficult to detect on Flat Coats because of their colour, but their bodies tend to shine. Also they leave a fine type of ash as excreta which can be seen in the coat. Fleas live by sucking blood which obviously sets up an irritation; the dog scratches and his hair comes out, sometimes sores will develop causing some quite nasty places. Treatment is by means of parasitic powders or sprays, or in bad cases a medicated bath may be necessary. It is also possible to buy a flea collar made by one of the proprietary firms for dog care and this protection lasts for several months. Hedgehogs are covered in fleas and if your dog finds one he is likely to be covered by them too, but as this particular type of flea does not use the dog as host they are fairly easily dealt with by the usual means.

GASTRITIS   This is colic or or violent indigestion and often occurs when a dog has bolted his food too fast; young pups are often the worst affected in this way. It can sometimes also occur if the dog is given cold food straight from the fridge. Our dogs often eat a certain type of coarse grass to make themselves vomit bile but it does not appear to do them any harm. If, however, the dog is always being sick the vet needs to be consulted as there may be something wrong.

HARD PAD   This disease is related to the distemper virus and got its name because it did, in fact, cause a hardening of the pads of the feet, but nowadays, by means of vaccination, much progress has been made and this condition is no longer so likely to occur.

HERNIAS   Usually found in puppies when the bitch has nipped off the navel cord too close to the puppy, although again it can be an inherited fault, particularly in bitches. I have had it occasionally in Flat Coat puppies when it has closed up of its own accord, but only once when it has been necessary to get the vet to operate. Hernias are the result of a weak place in the muscle in the tummy wall which forms a protrusion of the abdominal organs and causes a soft swelling.

HIP DYSPLASIA   Luckily this disease has, in the main, left our breed alone, although it has been known for young Flat Coats to suffer from Hip Dysplasia due to over exercising when bones are immature. It is most unusual to meet it in our breed as it is hereditary and in the past Flat Coated Retrievers have not been troubled with HD although both their cousins, the Goldens and Labradors have. HD is the condition in which the head of the femur (long leg bone) is out of shape and will not fit into the socket in the pelvis, causing the dog to have problems with his movement in very bad cases, although in most instances it is impossible to tell that a dog has got HD until it is X-rayed. This is done by your own vet (or arranged by the Society) once only and the scores sent to the British Veterinary Association for assessment. The X-ray is assessed on nine different parts of the hip joint, each leg separately; lowest scores best up to 6 on each $9 \times 6 = 54$ points for really bad HD giving 108 for both. A number of people believe that if a dog has not got the disease before the X-ray it will have afterwards as it is put out by injection and pulled about so much in order to get the photographs; they therefore will not have their dogs X-rayed at all. Lots of breeders shudder at the very words Hip Dysplasia, often thinking that affected dogs are in continual pain and are unable to get about, but as a general rule this is not the case and working ability is not impaired.

INNOCULATION I usually have my Flat Coat puppies innoculated against Distemper, Parvo and Hard Pad at about the age of twelve weeks for the first injection and a second one a fortnight later. After that I usually allow about four days for that injection to take effect before taking them out of the garden and yard where they have had the protection from their mother, to where other dogs have been roaming. The vets have several types of branded vaccine from which to choose and will issue a booklet giving dates etcetera and when to return for a booster shot in about a year's time. When going to the surgery I do not put my puppies down on the table or in fact anywhere at all on the vet's premises just in case they pick up something and, in fact, if you ask him, the vet will probably come out to the car to give the puppy a jab there.

JAUNDICE As with humans, dogs suffering from jaundice also go yellow around the eyes and inside the mouth from this condition. It is most usually caused by Weils Disease or Leptospiral Jaundice, which is transmitted by rats, either by an infected bite or by drinking water in which a rat has urinated, and affects the liver and kidneys. Some of the distemper vaccinations also cover against this disease which can prove fatal if not treated.

KENNEL COUGH This seems to have become a menace only in recent years and like the same disease in horses, can be transmitted, so if your Flat Coat has a husky, annoying, repetitive little cough, don't take him where there are others because it can infect a whole kennel. Should one bring it home the whole lot can get it and, although fit dogs are hardly affected, any that are under par, or very young, can be fatally pulled down, as there are no symptoms to speak of and thus people tend to treat it too lightly.

KIDNEY DISEASE (NEPHRITIS)   As dogs get old, and remember Flat Coats do not live to a great age, ten being about average, failure of the kidneys is one of the causes of having to put them down. When the kidneys stop acting as a filter for the waste products these go back into the blood stream and poisoning occurs which results in a terrible thirst, bad breath and vomiting, for which unfortunately there is only one answer. As I mentioned when talking about Jaundice, Nephritis can also be caused through Weils Disease which results in Leptospiral Kidney Disease, but this should respond to antibiotics.

LICE   These can be picked up from other dogs and are tiny round whitish parasites which live by attaching themselves to the dog's skin where they feed by sucking blood and then change colour. They are found in Flat Coats particularly around the ears, where they lay eggs or nits which look like scurf but are actually cemented to the hairs of the coat. One of the problems with these pests is that they can carry tapeworm eggs which become ingested and cause worms. Excessive scratching, particularly at the ears, is a sign and treatment is by means of a good spray or veterinary insecticidal shampoo.

MANGE   This is actually a living organism and is transmitted to both dogs and humans by contact with a dog with mange, or from infected bedding. There are two types of this parasitic skin disease, the most common being Sarcoptic Mange where the mite burrows under the skin to lay its eggs rather like Scabies in humans. This can be fairly easily cured but if left the inflammation can spread all over the body forming nasty scabs.

The second type is called Demodectic or Follicular Mange which is not transmissable, but because the mite lives right down in the deep layers of skin and can also probe the glandular system of the infected dog it is very much more difficult to get rid of. The condition can be inherited by the puppies from an infected bitch very early on in their lives which is why, if your Flat Coat bitch has had demodectic mange, it is much wiser not to breed from her at all. Severe irritation results from this condition and a peculiar musty odour is noticeable and if not treated abscesses are formed and septicaemia can set in.

MASTITIS   This condition most usually occurs in cows, but both humans and bitches can suffer from inflammation of the milk glands when suckling their young. It is extremely painful and the bitch will be off her food and running a temperature. In fact, once we nearly lost one of our bitches with mastitis. She was obviously in great pain and because the teat was not giving pure milk the puppies would not suck. The vet said he dare not open it because of infection, and we seemed to be at an impasse when Pandy solved it for herself by biting open the offending gland and licking out the clotted milk. However, it was noticeable that that particular teat did not seem to be able to be operative when the next litter came along.

PARVOVIRUS   Usually fatal. A very tough virus only recognised in dogs since 1978. It is caught from other dogs through virus excreted in faeces and from human shoes and clothing. Most often affecting puppies and youngsters up to one year old, it destroys the intestinal cell lining so the patient cannot absorb fluid and food. Fatalities are due to dehydration. It is difficult to eradicate in affected kennel.

POISONING   This is the cause of many dogs dying every year and most often it is from bait put down in the country by rat catchers or poachers which causes the trouble. Once we had Sam very ill and nearly lost him from Warfarin poisoning, and as there wasn't any on the place we could only think it must have been dropped by a bird. In towns dustbins are a great temptation to dogs and also a great source of potential danger. Although Warfarin is said to be harmless to pets, dogs like it and if taken in large amounts it can cause internal haemorrhages which can be fatal. Many of the modern weed killers and the strychnine that is sold for the purpose of getting rid of moles can have the same effect. To treat a dog you suspect of being poisoned you must first make it sick and the best way is to give a very strong solution of salt and water, then keep it warm until the vet comes.

PYOMETRA   This is a condition whereby the womb becomes infected with pus and most often occurs in bitches of middle age. This is the reason why many people, mistakenly, think they need to breed with their bitch the one-off litter so as to avoid this trouble. However, even bitches that have had puppies can suffer from it although it is unusual. My old lady, Woodwren, developed pyometra having had three litters previously, which the vet said was very unusual. Then Pandy (Rumaigne) having had five litters at the age of ten was successfully operated on. The condition occurs after a season and if the pus is able to drain away it looks very much like a continuation of the heat colour. It can be fatal and needs a hysterectomy, the sooner the better if you are to save your bitch and, in fact, it was only very prompt action by my vet that saved Sweep and Pandy to live to be plagued by their great-great-grandchildren.

RABIES (HYDROPHOBIA)   We hear so much about rabies these days with the disease almost up to the ports just across the channel. Some silly misguided people try to smuggle animals into this country instead of putting them into the statutory six months' quarantine. It is a very serious disease for which there is no cure and it is from animals like the dog and fox that it can be transmitted to man, when apart from the treatment being extremely painful it is invariably fatal. As I write, new rules have come into force concerning the export of puppies to the Continent and now Holland has come into line with Belgium and Germany and all require a rabies vaccination thirty days before the Flat Coat puppy leaves this country, so puppies being exported cannot now go to their new homes before twelve weeks of age unless they have had no infections at all when they can receive the necessary one the other side of the Channel.

SCURF   This is the appearance of dry scales on the coat and I have known it appear on dogs while waiting to go into the ring, almost as some sort of nervous condition. Nutmeg used to suffer from this when she was young but later did not seem to be affected so perhaps show familiarity breeds immunity; some vets think that centrally heated houses can be to blame for scurf appearing at regular intervals, especially when there is an almost continuous shedding of the coat. Puppies too sometimes get it, particularly if they have not been wormed and are out of condition, or it can be the result of not rinsing soap out of the coat properly after bathing, or even a tiny mite which is living on a puppy's skin. However, some forms of scurf are dry eczema and the vet needs consulting in both the latter cases.

TEETH   Your Flat Coat puppy will have the sharpest little needles in his mouth when he first arrives at his new home aged about eight weeks, but by the time he is six months old he should have gained a beautiful set of white permanent teeth that will stay in perfect condition if, like children, the dog is fed proper food, avoiding too many sweet things like chocolate and biscuits. The scissor bite is the correct mouth for a Flat Coat and dogs that have teeth that are undershot or overshot have bad faults and should not be used for breeding.

108

TICKS Living in the country has many advantages, but one of the disadvantages is that every now and again the dogs pick up ticks, very often from sheep. These parasites are white to start with, but they live by burying their heads in the dog's skin and sucking its blood, when they fill out and turn a blueish black enlarging to half an inch in diameter. They very often look like a cyst but a closer examination will show legs and a head. Don't try to pull them off or you can leave this head behind, which may form an abscess. They can be removed after applying cotton wool soaked in surgical spirit or disinfectant, and in any case will drop off in time when they have gorged themselves, but they are unsightly and cause irritation.

TRAVEL SICKNESS This is not actually an illness, although the dog who suffers from it can be very ill. Often it is brought on because of over-excitement at the start of a journey. As a general rule all our Flat Coats take to the car like ducks to water and the only one we have ever had trouble with was Teddy who simply would not settle down and insisted on standing up and roaming around. However, by dint of much patience in mopping-up operations and not feeding him when we were going on a journey, he eventually improved so that he was no trouble at all, but I must say I did wonder if we should ever manage to get him to the shows in the early stages. It is also possible to obtain travel sickness tablets from some of the proprietory brands of pet care firms, but I have not found these to be necessary if one starts with short trips, gradually lengthening them, and refrains from feeding for a couple of hours before the journey.

WORMS All animals suffer from worm infestation at various times during their life span and although one may clear them up before too long dogs easily become re-infected, particularly from sheep or rabbits, and the whole cycle starts again. There are two main types of worms to be found in this country (some countries like Africa have many more). There are roundworms and tapeworms which are found in the stomach and intestines, living on half-digested food. Roundworms are usually found in puppies and bitches in whelp. They are rather like a thinner edition of a white garden worm up to 8–9 inches in length and when treated and excreted look like lengths of spaghetti or chewed string. They are transmitted in the form of eggs found in the dog's droppings, ingested by licking, and the larvae develop in the stomach to form adult worms and the cycle starts again. When a bitch is pregnant, larvae that have lain dormant are activated by hormone production, and the puppies become infected even before birth through the blood stream. They need worming as early as three weeks, and then again at fortnightly intervals, because only the adult worms are killed by treatment and the newly hatched larvae have to be killed in their turn.

Under the title of Toxocara Canis there has been a great deal written and said about the danger to children of roundworm infection. This too can be gained through the ingestion of eggs which hatch out in the intestines and the larvae then travel to various parts of the body including the eyes and the brain. It can be seen that it is, therefore, vitally important that where children come into contact with puppies the latter must be wormed regularly, and all exretia picked up quickly to avoid the ground becoming infested with the roundworm eggs which can still be active for up to five years on the surface of the earth.

Adult dogs mostly suffer from tapeworm and we dose our dogs about three times a year as we have sheep running in the field next to the house at various times and they are one of the main hosts, for tapeworms have to have an intermediary stage. Tapeworms are white segments joined together with a head at the top which attaches itelf by means of hooks to the lining of the stomach or intestines. Single segments carrying eggs are excreted by the dog while still alive and wriggling, though they do die off once out of the body. The eggs are then picked up by birds, rabbits or fleas, transmitted to the dog by way of the mouth, grow into larvae and thence into tapeworms and the cycle is repeated. Thus if this parasite is to be eliminated the head must be got rid of or the whole business will begin again. This means that a dog needs dosing twice to be on the safe side and the best tablets are those obtained from your vet. Some people very occasionally give whole boiled apples, skin, cores and the lot, which is a very old remedy but some of these old cures are not to be sneezed at.

ZOONOSES This is the term applied to diseases which are transmissible from animals to humans. There is a minimal risk in the case of dogs, providing hygienic precautions are taken in dealing with food preparation and dishes, faeces are picked up regularly and properly disposed of and hands are washed after dealing with animals.

Sensible food, exercise, love and care go a long way towards having a fit and healthy Flat Coat, but everyone needs the vet's services at some time. In fact, the more dogs one keeps the more often this is necessary for obvious reasons, but visits can be kept to a minimum with some knowledge and a lot of commonsense.

10

Champions of the Breed

As explained earlier, the award of three Challenge Certificates under three separate judges will give a Flat Coat the title of Show Champion, providing at least one of these tickets has been won when the dog was over the age of twelve months. Being a gundog, to become a full champion he will then need to qualify in the field, either by getting an award of First, Second, Third or a Certificate of Merit at a field trial or qualify via the Show Gundog Working Certificate. These are held at certain field trial meetings where at least one of the judges is on the 'A' retriever judging list. The test usually takes place just before the break for lunch and the dog has to find and retrieve live game which is either shot or thrown specially for him. Notification of these field trials appears in the monthly Kennel Gazette and entry has to be made by the closing date for the trial.

Records of all wins of Challenge Certificates, Reserve Challenge Certificates or First, Second or Third places in Open or Limit classes at championship shows are shown in the Stud Book along with Field Trial, Working Trial and Test C Obedience class winners. The details registered on the pedigree of name, sex, colour, date of birth, owner, breeder and a three generation pedigree are listed and a number assigned to the dog under which this information is recorded for posterity. Published annually, the Stud Book is listed alphabetically under either Sporting or Non-Sporting subsections which are divided into the usual six groups. The first of the Stud Books were produced under the direction of the Kennel Club in 1874, a year after the Club's inception, and the man responsible for this onerous task was Mr Frank C. S. Pearce. He had a most difficult job, for in the early days, dogs were given pet names only and there were literally dozens of Besses and Bens, not to mention Sams and Sailors, and the only way to cope with this problem was to list the owners where they were known. This is the reason why there were so many dogs with unregistered parents in those early pedigrees. The Stud Book has been published yearly ever since the first issue and though sometimes late and sometimes, as in both World Wars, very thin in content, it provides the ongoing history of all those breeds recognised by the English canine authority.

Flat Coats were listed as Retrievers-Wavy Coated until 1898 when they became known as Flat Coated. They were by far the most numerous of the three retriever breeds until the outbreak of the Second World War after which they slipped down the popularity ratings.

Eight years after the first Stud Book appeared comes mention of a Flat Coat gaining a title. This was in 1882 and the bitch was Champion Mabel, sired by Merlin out of Maud on 6 May 1877 and bred by the Rev. Sergeantson. Also born in the same year was Ben, the first dog champion, by Shot out of Bena, the breeder being Mr E. G. Farquharson. Some other early Flat Coat breeders and their dogs were 1859 Mr Brailsford's Wyndham; 1867 Mr T. Hunt's Beauty; 1869 Admiral Curry's Sailor and Dr Bond Moore's Molière; 1870 Mr Palmer's Paris; 1872 J. D. Hull's Maude and the Rev. T.

Ch Shargleam Blackcap. (Photograph: David Dalton)

Darenth, the father of the present day Flat Coat, owned by Mr L. Allen Shuter (DOB 28.8.88).

Pearce's Hero; 1873 Mr Farquharson's Nero and J. D. Hull's Thorn plus in 1874 R. J. Lloyd Price's Comedy.

Stud Book entries these days are sent to one person in each breed who is knowledgeable about owners, pedigrees and shows and who proof-reads the computer sheets before they go into print. I check the Flat Coat entries and it is surprising the mistakes that can be found. In the old days, before this system was evolved, incorrect data was allowed to go through, with the result that one cannot be sure that the information given is completely accurate. One such mistake that I have found is in the entries for Black Cloth and his son, Black Drake, for according to the dates given in the Stud Book the son is a year older than his father.

Some of the well-known breeders in the early history of the Flat Coat who produced a number of champions were S. E. Shirley (seven), W. J. Phizacklea (twelve) and H. R. Cooke (ten), but it must not be forgotten that the Society owes an enormous debt to such people as Colin Wells, who has had twelve 'W' champions to my certain knowledge (nine of which were dogs) and Dr Nancy Laughton with six from her Claverdon kennel who kept the breed alive during the dark days of 1939–1945.

The list of Champions recorded in this chapter is as complete as I can make it and although the Kennel Club did not grant the title of Show Champion until 1958 I have listed all those early dogs who gained three Challenge Certificates before that date as the Kennel Club agreed to allow their claim to a title to be recognised. Pre-war, more bitches than dogs became Show Champions although more dogs became full champions. Today, honours are about even.

It is most interesting tracing pedigrees and one I have on the wall incites a great deal of interest from visitors. It is in the shape of a round ten generation pedigree showing the family tree of my original brood bitch, Woodwren; covering 2,600 names it dates back to 1912. If you, the reader, should be interested in producing one for yourself you will need to spend some considerable time checking through old Stud Books or, if you don't mind cheating a bit, contact Jill Saville, 280 West Parade, Lincoln, who has spent a great deal of time collecting and collating Flat Coat pedigrees solely for the benefit of breed enthusiasts.

I hope the information contained within this chapter will whet a few appetites and will help the reader to gain a little knowledge of his or her own dog's family tree.

DARENTH'S PEDIGREE

PARENTS	GRAND-PARENTS	G.G.-PARENTS	G.G.G.-PARENTS	G.G.G.G.-PARENTS
SIRE CH HOPEFUL	**SIRE** HARVESTER KC No 17024	**SIRE** FROLIC 12629	**SIRE** CH DUSK 6297	Thorn Late Bit / Lady in Black
			DAM TUNE 9228	Thorn / Melody
		DAM LADY IN BLACK	**SIRE** PRINCE	Lyon or Hercules / Bess (Imp Lansdown)
			DAM LADY BONNIE	Windham 1587 / Jumbo Bonnie 1681
	DAM THINK	**SIRE** CH DUSK	**SIRE** THORN	Victor / Yuvie Bonnie
			DAM LADY IN BLACK	Pris / Lady Bonnie
		DAM WISDOM	**SIRE** MOLIERE	Worcestershire / ―
			DAM MAUD	Wyndham / Jumbo Bonnie
DAM DONNA	**SIRE** CH MOONSTONE	**SIRE** CH ZEPSTONE	**SIRE** CH BEN	Shot / Bonna
			DAM BRIDGET	Tuck / Nellis II
		DAM THINK	**SIRE** CH DUSK	Thorn / Lady in Black
			DAM WISDOM	Moliere / Maud
	DAM VENICE	**SIRE** SAM	**SIRE** FRANK	Mono / Seen
			DAM MABEL	Nell / Merlin
		DAM BEVA	**SIRE** NERO	Mabel / Fats
			DAM BOX	Frout / Worcestershire

I certify this Pedigree to be correct to the best of my knowledge

Signed .... Date ....

Printed by Dog Breeders Associates

Five generation pedigree of Darenth.

115

DOG CHAMPIONS

Dog	Date of Birth	Sire	Dam	Breeder
Ch Ben	1877	Shot	Bena	E. G. Farquharson
Ch Dusk	June 1877	Thorn	Lady in Black	S. E. Shirley
Ch Zelstone	8 March 1880	Ch Ben	Bridget	E. G. Farquharson
Ch Moonstone	7 March 1882	Ch Zelstone	Think	S. E. Shirley
Ch Black Thorn	4 April 1884	Ch Moonstone	Sloe	Maj Harding Cox & M. Jaquet
Ch Hopeful	19 January 1886	Harvester	Think	S. E. Shirley
Ch Wiseacre	11 February 1887	Ch Zelstone	Think	S. E. Shirley
Ch Taut	17 September 1888	Windward	Rivington Gipsy	Mr Phillips
Ch Darenth	28 December 1888	Ch Hopeful	Donna	L. A. Shuter
Ch Blizzard	2 May 1891	Ch Darenth	Breeze	Col H. C. Legh
Ch Black Cloth	25 June 1895	Ch Darenth	Black Skirt	Maj Harding Cox
Ch Pettings Mallard	8 November 1895	Ch Darenth	Pettings Mop	J. G. Hulkes
Ch Black Drake	10 December 1896	Ch Black Cloth	Black Paint	Maj Harding Cox
Ch Wimpole Peter	25 May 1897	Ch Black Drake	Racket	F. Keen
Ch Horton Rector	2 February 1899	Ch Darenth	Black Blossom	L. A. Shuter
Ch Black Quilt	18 July 1900	Ch Horton Rector	Ch Black Queen	Maj Harding Cox
Ch Paul of Riverside	17 July 1901	Ch Wimpole Peter	Ch Worsley Bess	H. R. Cooke
Ch High Legh Blarney	18 February 1902	Ch Black Quilt	High Legh Moment	Lt Col H. Cornwall
Ch Sandy of Riverside	1 June 1902	Mountain Sam	Tyncefn Jet	G. Campbell
Ch Shotover	8 March 1903	Ch Black Quilt	Queen of Llangollen	P. Heaton
Ch Royal River	30 December 1903	Ch Paul of Riverside	Sweet Fern	L. A. Shuter
Ch Rocket of Riverside	11 January 1904	Ch Paul of Riverside	Tyncefn Set	G. Campbell
Ch Longshaw Bruce	24 June 1906	Ch High Legh Blarney	Longshaw Duchess	E. Ashton
Ch Jimmy of Riverside	22 September 1906	Ch High Legh Blarney	Duchess	H. R. Cooke
Ch Wrangler	19 March 1909	Horton Viceroy	Wilful	G. Tree
Ch Roddy of Riverside	19 April 1909	Ch Rocket of Riverside	Rachel	J. H. Abbott
Ch Kaffir of Riverside	29 April 1909	Ch High Legh Blarney	Lambton Kitty	C. Porch

Name	Date			Owner
Ch Southwell Peter	30 June 1910	Southwell Abbott	Ch Southwell Dolly Varden	Lt Col Le Marchant & G. H. & T. S. Elliott
Sh Ch Leecroft Minor	1 June 1912	Ch Longshaw Bruce	Leecroft Marjorie	E. Ashton
Sh Ch Pike	20 March 1913	Ch Wrangler	Gipsy of Trewern	S. H. Burrows
Ch Towerwood Vigour	11 February 1920	Hollingbourne Help	Towerwood Duchess	W. Skerry
Sh Ch Leecroft Buxton	31 January 1921	Leecroft Young Prince	Triumph Tess	G. W. P. Beswick
Ch Dandie of Shipton	29 January 1922	Darkie of Riverside	Bank Burr	N. G. Badham
Ch Tosca Dazzler	16 May 1922	Jock of Riverside	Tosca Biddy	H. R. Cooke
Ch Boughton Diver	8 February 1923	Darkie of Riverside	Stretton Dark Night	Mr Davies
Sh Ch Leecroft Peter	10 August 1924	Sh Ch Leecroft Buxton	Foxlow Dolly	G. W. P. Beswick
Ch Dander of Riverside	16 May 1925	Ch Tosca Dazzler	Trout of Riverside	A. Hull
Sh Ch Bridgelea Banker (late Oxmead Ace)	20 June 1925	Birchinlee Ted	Doveside Nell	A. Ravensdale
Sh Ch Dipper of Riverside	5 May 1926	Ch Tosca Dazzler	Puffin of Riverside	A. Hull
Ch Specialist	11 June 1928	David	Spark	A. E. Southam
Ch Mate of Riverside	11 March 1929	Ch Dancer of Riverside	Ch Atherbram Jet	W. J. Phizacklea
Ch Flapper of Riverside	16 April 1929	Toddy of Riverside	Polly of Riverside	H. R. Cooke
Ch Atherbram Prince	13 November 1930	Ch Dancer of Riverside	Ch Atherbram Jet	W. J. Phizacklea
Ch Kipper of Riverside	13 November 1930	Ch Dancer of Riverside	Ch Atherbram Jet	W. J. Phizacklea
Ch Whin of Riverside	19 July 1931	David	Swanbourne Flirt	H. R. Cooke
Ch Peddars Boy	4 May 1932	Noddy of Riverside	Towerwood Dawn	W. Skerry
Ch Aerodyne	15 February 1934	Ch Specialist	Speck	A. E. Southam
Ch Merry Harmony	15 February 1934	Ch Specialist	Speck	A. E. Southam
Ch Karla Rat of Adlington	18 April 1935	Spar	Spero	A. E. Southam
Ch Peddars Drake	6 July 1936	Ch Atherbram Prince	Ch Peddars Lass	F. T. Allen
Ch Woodlark of Riverside	12 August 1936	Ch Whin of Riverside	Ch Kiss of Riverside	H. R. Cooke
Ch Waterman	1 February 1945	Atherbram Simon	Atherbram Meg	W. J. Phizacklea
Ch Atherbram Nobbie	14 April 1945	Atherbram Monty	Atherbram Bridget	W. J. Phizacklea
Ch Patricia's Bruce	14 October 1945	Atherbram Monty	Princess of Glascote	A. E. Bath
Ch Shot of Forestholm	1 May 1946	Atherbram Monty	Trout	J. Dyson

DOG CHAMPIONS

Dog	Date of Birth	Sire	Dam	Breeder
Ch Roland Tann	20 June 1947	Atherbram Jackie	Ch Dorfield Judith	E. Rowlands
Sh Ch Forestholm Blackcock	24 December 1948	Shot of Forestholm	Forestholm Jill of Holmland	Mrs P. M. Barwise
Ch Pewcroft Plug	26 April 1949	Bryn of Adlington	Pewcroft Peg	Stanley O'Neil
Ch Waterboy	4 May 1950	Ch Waterman	Claverdon Faith	Colin Wells
Ch Black Lion Rex of Ibaden	9 May 1950	Nobby of Riverside	Ch Flash of Ibaden	G. F. Wells
Ch Watchman	19 February 1952	Ch Waterman	Claverdon Faith	Colin Wells
Ch Workman	19 February 1952	Ch Waterman	Claverdon Faith	Colin Wells
Ch Atherbram Pedro	28 February 1952	Nobby of Riverside	Ch Atherbram Rosebud	Mrs F. E. Kearsley
Sh Ch Lydisdale Lancer of Ardagh	31 May 1953	Pewcroft Pieman	Flint of Claverdon	W. Worby
Ch Adonis	9 June 1955	Ch Waterboy	Ch Pewcroft Proper	Reed Flowers
Ch Pewcroft Prospector	26 November 1955	Claverdon Pegasus	Ch Pewcroft Picture	Mrs K. S. O'Neil
Ch Forestholm Donard	5 August 1956	Sh Ch Forestholm Blackcock	Woodland Picture	Mr McCleary
Ch Claverdon Jorricks of Willing	27 March 1957	Pewcroft Page	Ch Claverdon Powderbox	Mrs J. Wood
Ch Pewcroft Pitcher	7 May 1957	Denmere Bruce	Ch Pewcroft Pitch	Mrs K. S. O'Neil
Ch Woodlark	20 October 1958	Ch Waterboy	Ch Claverdon Tawny Pippet	Colin Wells
Ch Claverdon Comet	1 March 1959	Bob of Riverglade	Claverdon Turtledove	Dr N. Laughton
Ch Rungles Wag	27 September 1959	Waterboy of Springon	Ch Happy Wanderer	Mrs Fletcher & 'Tinker' Davis
Sh Ch Shadyoak Defender	15 November 1959	Ch Pewcroft Picture	Nesfield Shadyoak	Mrs L. Kent
Ch Strathendrick Shadow	27 May 1960	Ch Claverdon Jorrocks of Willing	Claverdon Bronte	J. Steven

Name	Date	Sire	Dam	Owner
Sh Ch Strathendrick Haze	18 August 1962	Ch Strathendrick Shadow	Claverdon Veracity	J. Steven
Ch Stolford Whinchat	30 August 1962	Blakeholme Jem	Ch Claverdon Tawny Pippet	Colin Wells
Ch Collyers Blakeholme Brewster	4 December 1962	Blakeholme Jem	Rettendon Spoonbill	Miss C. B. Hall
Ch Waveman	11 September 1963	Blakeholme Jem	Ch Wave	Colin Wells
Ch Downstream Hercules	1 November 1963	Winkswood	Downstream Pax	Mrs Shirley Johnson
Sh Ch Stolford Black Knight	29 December 1963	Ch Stolford Whinchat	Sh Ch Stolford Hartshorn Memory	Mrs Peggy Robertson
Sh Ch Sandylands Challenge	24 March 1964	Ch Claverdon Comet	Sh Ch Sandylands Rungles Witch	Mrs Gwen Broadley
Ch Fenrivers Golden Rod	23 May 1964	Ch Woodlark	Fenrivers Evergreen	Reed Flowers
Int Ch Donovan	22 April 1965	Ch Woodlark	Halstock Deliah	Colin Wells
Sh Ch Longforgan Black Shadow	31 July 1965	Pride of Achnacarry	Fenrivers Waterlily	George Lackie
Ch Ryshot Copper Ablaze	11 September 1965	Ryshot Copper Beau	Ryshot Copper Realm	Mrs Margaret Izzard
Ch Tonggreen Sparrow Boy	5 September 1966	Ch Fenrivers Golden Rod	Tonggreen Swift	Miss Joan Chester-Perks
Ch Bordercot Stolford Doonigan	10 November 1967	Int Ch Donovan	Ch Stolford Wychmere Black Seal	Mrs Peggy Robertson
Ch Woodway	1 February 1968	Int Ch Donovan	Ch Woodpoppy	Colin Wells
Ch Courtbeck Mercury	15 February 1968	Ch Claverdon Comet	Halstock Joanna	Miss Helen Beckwith
Ch Belsud Courtbeck Taurus	15 February 1968	Ch Claverdon Comet	Halstock Joanna	Miss Helen Beckwith
Sh Ch Oakmoss Ambassador	15 April 1968	Ch Fenrivers Golden Rod	Halstock Juliette	George & Mavis Lancaster
Ch Hallbent Gipsy Lad	25 July 1968	Ch Fenrivers Golden Rod	Hallbent Happy Wanderer	Miss G. Buchanan

DOG CHAMPIONS

Dog	Date of Birth	Sire	Dam	Breeder
Am Ch Couallenby Remus	1 May 1969	Ch Fenrivers Golden Rod	Halstock Delia	Mrs D. P. Mathews
Sh Ch Can & Am Ch Parkburn Brandy Boy	14 April 1969	Lysander of Tamara	Leah of Tamara	Mrs M. Jewell
Sh Ch Woodman	26 September 1969	Ch Tonggreen Sparrow Boy	Ch Woodpoppy	Colin Wells
Ch Wizardwood Sandpiper	29 January 1971	Ch Tonggreen Sparrow Boy	Halstock Jemima of Wizardwood Woodwren	Mr & Mrs P. Forster
Sh Ch Rase Romulus	25 November 1971	Ch Hallbent Gipsy Lad	Windgather Delia of Wizardwood	Mrs Paddy Petch
Ch Wizardwood Teal	8 October 1972	Ch Wizardwood Sandpiper		Mr & Mrs P. Forster
Ch Damases Tarquol of Ryshot	14 January 1973	Ch Tonggreen Sparrow Boy	Hallbent Contessa	Mrs J. Green
Ch Exclyst Bernard	7 March 1973	Nor Ch Halstock Lone Ranger	Wyndhamian Claudette	Mrs B. Phillips
Ch Monarch of Leurbost	28 July 1973	Braden of Longforgan	Halstock Louisa	Jimmy Boyd
Ch Am & Can Ch Parkburn Dextensing of Casuarina	2 February 1974	Sh Ch Can & Am Ch Parkburn Brandy Boy	Can Ch The Parc Dawn	Mrs M. Jewell
Ch Tonggreen Squall	29 March 1974	Tonggreen Starling	Ch Leahador Dusk of Tonggreen	Miss J. Chester-Perks
Ch Puhfuh Phineas Finn CDEX WDEX WD	20 April 1974	Wyndhamian Christopher of Exclyst	Linda of Puhfuh	Mrs Joan Shore
Ch Belsud Black Buzzard	1 June 1974	Ch Belsud Courtbeck Taurus	Belsud Black Guillemot	Mrs Mary Grimes
Sh Ch Wizardwood Hawfinch	24 August 1975	Claverdon Juliet	Sh Ch Alicia of Wizardwood	Mr & Mrs P. Forster

Name	Date	Sire	Dam	Owner
Ch Stantilaine Rory of Branchalwood	22 October 1975	Kenstaff Whipster	Glendaruel Christina	Mrs S. Telfer
Ch Greinton Dugald	30 August 1976	Ch Damases Tarquol of Ryshot	Braidwyn Brigadoon of Greinton	Mrs J. Small
Sh Ch Nortonwood Black Bart	31 January 1977	Yonday Marshall	Stolford Chanelle	Mr & Mrs R. Bradbury
Ch & Ir Ch Shargleam Blackcap	26 June 1977	Ch Damases Tarquol of Ryshot	Ch Yonday Willow Warbler of Shargleam	Miss P. Chapman
Sh Ch Hallbent Kim	5 July 1978	Claverdon Kim	Hallbent Melody	Miss G. Buchanan
Ch Exclyst Imperial Mint	14 October 1978	Ch Belsud Black Buzzard	Ch Elizabeth of Exclyst	Mrs B. Phillips
Ch Bordercot Guy	30 December 1978	Sh Ch Nortonwood Black Bart	Sh Ch Vbos Vogue	W. Galloway
Ch Shargleam Sparrowhawk	4 September 1979	Wizardwood Tawny Owl	Shargleam Bunting	Miss P. Chapman
Ch Falswift Apparition	29 December 1979	Ch & Ir Ch Shargleam Blackcap	Ch Halstock Primula of Ravenscrest	Mrs P. Westrop
Sh Ch Emanon Parkgate Boy	14 May 1980	Kenjo Black Knight	Ch Halstock Bridget	Mrs P. Miller
Ch Withybed Country Lad	5 September 1980	Ch Tonggreen Squall	Ch Shargleam Black Abby of Withybed	Mr & Mrs R. Adams
Sh Ch Maybrian Trailblazer	13 April 1981	Ch & Ir Ch Shargleam Blackcap	Maybrian Ballerina	Mr & Mrs B. Pash
Ch Torwood Blue	25 July 1981	Torwood Jolly	Bowmore Traddles Girl of Torwood	Mr & Mrs N. Jury
Sh Ch Blue Boy of Braidwyn	14 September 1981	Braidwynn Chancellor	Vbos Velour	Mr & Mrs E. R. Smith
Sh Ch Heronsflight Pan's Promise	18 April 1982	Glenwherry Oak	Heronsflight Pansy	Mrs J. Mason & Mrs R. Talbot
Sh Ch Shargleam Fieldfare	2 August 1982	Ch Withybed Country Lad	Shargleam Bunting	Miss P. Chapman
Sh Ch Shargleam Kingfisher	23 March 1983	Ch & Ir Ch Shargleam Blackcap	Sh Ch Withybed Country Girl of Shargleam	Miss P. Chapman

BITCH CHAMPIONS

Bitch	Date of Birth	Sire	Dam	Breeder
Ch Mabel	May 1877	Merlin	Maud	The Rev. Sergeantson
Ch Sloe	2 March 1879	Thorn	Lady in Black	S. E. Shirley
Ch Zee	7 March 1882	Zelstone	Think	S. E. Shirley
Ch Tacit	27 March 1883	Zelstone	Think	S. E. Shirley
Ch Black Queen	12 April 1893	Ch Black Drake	Racket	F. Keene
Ch Kite	16 March 1894	Buoyant	Kale	The Duke of Buccleuch
Ch Worsley Bess	28 March 1894	Barton Zulu	Trinket	G. Cook
Ch Bring 'Em	12 February 1900	Ch Black Drake	Squib	W. G. Badham
Ch Sweet Fern	22 March 1901	Ch Horton Rector	Horton Brackern	L. A. Shuter
Ch Gipsy of Riverside	6 April 1902	Ch Wimpole Peter	Maid of Llangollen	H. R. Cooke
Ch Bank Bess	12 February 1903	Ch Paul of Riverside	Squib	W. G. Badham
Ch Judy of Riverside	14 April 1903	Ch Black Quilt	Duchess	H. R. Cooke
Sh Ch Wigeon of River- side	28 February 1906	Ch High Legh Blarney	Bank Book	H. R. Cooke
Ch Bank Betty	1 March 1907	Ch Locket of Riverside	Bank Book	W. G. Badham
Ch Blossom of Riverside	15 August 1907	Ch Rocket of Riverside	Ch Judy of Riverside	W. G. Badham
Ch Bianca	25 April 1908	Hermit	Bank Book	W. G. Badham
Ch Southwell Dolly	1 August 1908	Ch High Legh Blarney	Southwell Nell	Lt Col Le Marchant & G. H. & T. S. Elliott
Ch Mollance Meg	22 January 1911	Ch Jimmy of Riverside	Witness	J. B. Nelson
Sh Ch Mereside Nancy	2 September 1911	Ch Wrangler	Withington Nell	J. H. Hulme
Sh Ch Seagull	26 March 1914	Roger of Mereside	Utica	A. E. Southam
Sh Ch Joan of Riverside	7 June 1919	Madeley Major	Dye of Agden	J. Fox
Sh Ch Nun of Riverside	20 May 1920	Mole of Riverside	Dye of Agden	J. Fox
Ch Kennet Doris	25 May 1920	Perch of Riverside	Dora	R. H. Hersey
Ch Longstone Jet	30 August 1920	Leecroft Marne	Mischief	W. Rowbotham
Ch Breeze of Riverside	1 August 1921	Knight of Riverside	Seaweed	A. J. Moore

122

Name	Date	Sire	Dam	Owner
Sh Ch Trout of Riverside	14 February 1922	Jock of Riverside	Rhona	E. Simmons
Sh Ch Spark	18 February 1923	Birchdale Jimmy	Spratt	A. E. Southam
Sh Ch Betty of Riverside	6 August 1923	Jock of Riverside	Gyp	G. Dooley
Ch Tosca British Maid	3 March 1925	Blackdale Luke	Tosca Beauty	W. Simms
Ch Atherbram Jet	3 May 1925	Leecroft Buxton	Atherbram Biddy	W. J. Phizacklea
Ch Enmore Beth	21 March 1927	Ch Dandie of Shipton	Wellon	G. Smith
Ch Enmore Betty	21 March 1927	Ch Dandie of Shipton	Wellon	G. Smith
Sh Ch Nancy of Riverside	4 June 1929	Ch Dancer of Riverside	Nodfa	H. R. Cooke
Ch Kiss of Riverside	13 November 1930	Ch Dancer of Riverside	Ch Atherbram Jet	W. J. Phizacklea
Sh Ch Kale of Riverside	13 November 1930	Ch Dancer of Riverside	Ch Atherbram Jet	W. J. Phizacklea
Sh Ch Kitty of Riverside	13 November 1930	Ch Dancer of Riverside	Ch Atherbram Jet	W. J. Phizacklea
Ch Peddars Lass	15 February 1934	Ch Specialist	Speck	A. E. Southam
Ch Stainton Spinster	18 April 1935	Spar	Spero	A. E. Southam
Sh Ch Greta of Riverside	5 June 1935	Quick of Riverside	Sh Ch Nancy of Riverside	H. R. Cooke
Ch Peddars Bramble	6 July 1936	Ch Atherbram Prince	Ch Peddars Lass	F. T. Allen
Ch Claverdon Jet	11 March 1944	Atherbram Gunner	Cemlyn	W. J. Phizacklea
Ch Oathill Sheila	14 April 1945	Atherbram Monty	Atherbram Bridget	W. J. Phizacklea
Ch Lili Marlene	19 October 1945	Atherbram Monty	Atherbram Gill	W. J. Phizacklea
Ch Atherbram Rosebud	24 April 1947	Ch Atherbram Nobbie	Atherbram Gyp	W. J. Phizacklea
Ch Flash of Ibaden	7 December 1947	Ch Waterman	Ch Lili Marlene	Mr Mansfield
Ch Watchful	20 February 1948	Ch Waterman	Claverdon Faith	Dr N. Laughton
Ch Claverdon Black Velvet	20 February 1948	Ch Waterman	Claverdon Faith	Dr N. Laughton
Ch Claverdon Black Satin	5 March 1948	Revival of Ettington	Ch Claverdon Jet	Dr N. Laughton
Ch Pewcroft Pitch	26 April 1949	Bryn of Adlington	Pewcroft Peg	Stanley O'Neil
Ch Claverdon Miss Tinker	1 January 1950	Ch Atherbram Nobbie	Claverdon Celeste	Dr N. Laughton

BITCH CHAMPIONS

Bitch	Date of Birth	Sire	Dam	Breeder
Ch Claverdon Powderbox	3 May 1951	Ch Waterman	Ch Claverdon Jet	Dr N. Laughton
Ch Claverdon Waternymph	12 July 1951	Ch Waterman	Claverdon Faith	Dr N. Laughton
Ch Pewcroft Picture	24 March 1952	Sweep of Riverside	Pewcroft Peg	Stanley O'Neil
Ch Pewcroft Proper	5 April 1953	Denmere Prince	Ch Pewcroft Pitch	Stanley O'Neil
Ch Ryshot Misty Dawn	26 January 1955	Ryshot Peddars Reverie	Ryshot Starlight	Mrs Margaret Izzard
Ch Happy Wanderer	26 February 1955	Watchman	Sooty of Castle Park	A. V. Lee
Ch Claverdon Tawny Pippet	20 May 1955	Claverdon Pewcroft Pieman	Ch Claverdon Powderbox	Dr N. Laughton
Ch Asperula	9 June 1955	Ch Waterboy	Ch Pewcroft Proper	Reed Flowers
Ch Wave	1 February 1957	Ch Workman	Ch Claverdon Tawny Pippet	Colin Wells
Ch Ryshot Copper Bracken	6 March 1957	Forestholm Coppercoat of Ryshot	Sharpthorn Zepher	Mrs Richardson
Ch Pewcroft Prop of Yarlaw	7 May 1957	Denmere Bruce	Ch Pewcroft Pitch	Stanley O'Neil
Sh Ch Hollowdale Wendy	9 January 1959	Ch Claverdon Jorrocks of Lilling	Atherbram Tansy	Mrs Teasdale
Sh Ch Rungles Lady Barbara	27 September 1959	Waterboy of Springon	Ch Happy Wanderer	Mrs Fletcher & 'Tinker' Davis
Sh Ch Sandylands Rungles Witch	27 September 1959	Waterboy of Springon	Ch Happy Wanderer	Mrs Fletcher & 'Tinker' Davis
Sh Ch Fredwell Rungles Happy Wendy	27 September 1959	Waterboy of Springon	Ch Happy Wanderer	Mrs Fletcher & 'Tinker' Davis
Sh Ch Halstock Black Jewel	31 March 1960	Ryshot Rungles Trademark	Halstock Dinah	Mrs P. Lock

Name	Date	Sire	Dam	Owner
Ch Stolford Hartshorn Memory	3 February 1961	Ch Woodlark	Nesfield Stratton	Wilson Stephens
Sh Ch Blackbird of Yarlaw	15 May 1962	Ch Woodlark	Ch Pewcroft Prop of Yarlaw	Mrs C. T. Hutton
Sh Ch Blakeholme Joanna	4 December 1962	Blakeholme Jem	Rettingdon Spoonbill	Miss C. B. Hall
Ch Downstream Caliope	1 November 1963	Ch Woodman	Downstream Halstock Hussey	Mrs S. Johnson
Ch Ryshot Velvet	19 April 1964	Ryshot Mascot	Ryshot Copper Jacynth	Mrs Margaret Izzard
Ch Heronsflight Black Bell of Yarlaw	20 April 1964	Claverdon Jorrocks Junior	Ch Pewcroft Prop of Yarlaw	Mrs R. Hutton
Sh Ch Leighfoss Rungles Breeze	2 June 1964	Claverdon Jorrocks Junior	Sh Ch Rungles Lady Barbara	Mrs Fletcher & 'Tinker' Davis
Sh Ch Halstock Joanna	5 July 1964	Ch Stolford Whinchat	Sh Ch Black Jewel	Mrs P. Lock
Ch Woodpoppy	29 May 1965	Ch Woodlark	Hartshorn Sweetbriar	Colin Wells
Ch Stolford Wychmere Black Seal	6 October 1965	Ch Fenrivers Golden Rod	Stolford Black Pearl	R. Stead
Ch Blakeholme Just So	14 April 1966	Ch Fenrivers Golden Rod	Blakeholme Jenet	Miss C. B. Hall
Ch Black Fritta of Yarlaw	21 March 1967	Hartshorn Samphire	Black Lass of Yarlaw	Air Com W. Hutton
Ch Claverdon Fidelity	14 April 1967	Teal of Hawksnest	Claverdon Rhapsody	Dr N. Laughton
Ch Ryshot Idyll	27 September 1967	Ryshot Conquest	Ch Ryshot Velvet	Mrs Margaret Izzard
Ch Fenrivers Kalmia	27 December 1967	Ch Tonggreen Sparrow Boy	Blakeholme Juliet	Reed Flowers
Ch Stolford Mrs Mopp	14 February 1968	Ch Stolford Whinchat	Sh Ch Stolford Hartshorn Memory	Mrs P. Robertson
Ch Tonggreen Court-beck Venus	15 February 1968	Ch Claverdon Comet	Halstock Joanna	Miss H. Beckwith
Ch Kilbucho Honeybee	11 June 1968	Sh Ch Strathendrick Haze	Fenrivers Honeysuckle	Mrs D. Montgomery
Sh Ch Hallbent Teal	14 June 1969	Ch Fenrivers Golden Rod	Hallbent Happy Wanderer	Miss G. Buchanan

BITCH CHAMPIONS

Bitch	Date of Birth	Sire	Dam	Breeder
Sh Ch Halstock Alicia of Wizardwood	1 October 1969	Halstock Echo	Rungles Brilla	Mrs P. Miller
Ch Ryshot Copper Ring O'Fire	9 January 1970	Ch Ryshot Copper Ablaze	Ch Ryshot Idyll	Mrs Margaret Izzard
Ch Hallbent New Novel	6 May 1970	Hallbent Woodcock	Hallbent Dusk	Miss G. Buchanan
Ch Heronsflight Sedge	9 May 1970	Ch Tonggreen Sparrow Boy	Ch Heronsflight Black Bell of Yarlaw	Mrs J. Mason
Ch Leahador Dusk of Tonggreen	29 January 1971	Ch Hallbent Gipsy Lad	Leah of Tamara	Mrs D. Mitchell Innes
Sh Ch Vbos Velma	17 March 1971	Ch Tonggreen Sparrow Boy	Vbos Stolford Inkspot	Miss V. Ogilvy Shepherd
Ch Flowerdown Ebony Sonata	8 April 1971	Tonggreen Starling	Ryshot Copper Lyric	J. Preston
Ch Yonday Merry Maid	10 May 1971	Ch Courtbeck Mercury	Claverdon Flapper	Flt Lt G. Snape
Ch Andromeda of Kempton	31 July 1971	Tonggreen Starling	Belsud Linnet	Mrs J. Neal Smith
Sh Ch Tonggreen Song Linnet	15 September 1971	Ch Tonggreen Sparrow Boy	Ch Tonggreen Courtbeck Venus	Miss Joan Chester-Perks
Ch Rase Rumaigne	25 November 1971	Ch Hallbent Gipsy Lad	Woodwren	Mrs Paddy Petch
Sh Ch Belsud Magpie	27 July 1972	Tonggreen Starling	Belsud Black Guillemot	Mrs M. Grimes
Ch Wizardwood Wigeon	8 October 1972	Ch Wizardwood Sandpiper	Windgather Delia of Wizardwood	Mr & Mrs P. Forster
Sh Ch Damases Tara	14 January 1975	Ch Tonggreen Sparrow Boy	Hallbent Contessa	Mrs J. Green
Sh Ch Rase Pipestrelle	7 March 1974	Ch Bordercot Stolford Doonigan	Sh Ch Rase Rumaigne	Mrs Paddy Petch

Name	Date	Sire	Dam	Owner
Ch Yonday Willow Warbler of Shargleam	7 June 1974	Kenstaff Whipster	Claverdon Flapper	Flt Lt G. Snape
Sh Ch Vbos Vogue	9 March 1975	Ch Bordercot Stolford Doonigan	Sh Ch Vbos Velma	Miss V. Ogilvy Shepherd
Ch Elizabeth of Exclyst	12 June 1975	Wyndhamian Christopher of Exclyst	Shirelf of Ryshot	Mrs J. Durman
Ch Wizardwood Brown Owl	21 July 1975	Fenrivers Ling	Windgather Delia of Wizardwood	Mr & Mrs P. Forster
Ch Halstock Primula of Ravenscrest	6 January 1975	Wyndhamian Christopher of Exclyst	Halstock Stargirl	Mrs P. Lock
Sh Ch Tormick Ash	15 January 1975	Komati Poort	Crackodawn Bush Baby	M. T. Freeman
Sh Ch Wizardwood Little Owl	21 July 1975	Fenrivers Ling	Windgather Delia of Wizardwood	Mr & Mrs P. Forster
Ch Stantilaine Garnet of Glendaruel	22 October 1975	Kenstaff Whipster	Glendaruel Christina	Mrs Telfer
Ch Midnight Star of Exclyst	27 July 1976	Wyndhamian Christopher of Exclyst	Shirelf of Ryshot	Mrs J. Durman
Sh Ch Fabiennes Katoomba	10 November 1976	Sh Ch Wizardwood Hawfinch	Rase Phoenix of Fabiennes	Mrs F. Thomas
Ch Halstock Bridget	5 April 1977	Ch Belsud Black Buzzard	Halstock Magnolia	Mrs P. Lock
Ch Shargleam Black Abby of Withybed	26 June 1977	Ch Damases Tarquol of Ryshot	Ch Yonday Willow Warbler of Shargleam	Miss P. Chapman
Ch Branchalwood Frisa	25 August 1977	Ch Tonggreen Squall	Branchalwood Maree	Mr & Mrs Scott Dalziel
Ch Torwood Poppet	27 August 1977	Heronsflight Tercel	Heronsflight Puff	Mr & Mrs N. Jury
Ch Palnure Pride of Branchalwood	24 June 1978	Ch Tonggreen Squall	Branchalwood Linnie	Mrs A. Dimmock
Ch Larg Linnet of Pendlewych	24 June 1978	Ch Tonggreen Squall	Branchalwood Linnie	Mrs A. Dimmock
Ch Nashville Dawn of Sedgedunum	17 August 1978	Ch Tonggreen Squall	Vbos Vonda	Mrs Wotherspoon

BITCH CHAMPIONS

Bitch	Date of Birth	Sire	Dam	Breeder
Ch Black Velvet of Candidacasa at Waverton	30 December 1978	Sh Ch Nortonwood Black Bart	Vbos Vogue	W. Galloway
Ch Tonggreen Swift Lark of Shargleam	12 December 1979	Ch & Ir Ch Shargleam Blackcap	Tonggreen Song Swift	Mrs P. Cowley & Miss J. Chester-Perks
Ch Belsud Brown Guillemot	6 June 1979	Ch Exclyst Bernard	Belsud Blackcap	Mrs M. Grimes
Ch Falswift Auriga	29 December 1979	Ch & Ir Ch Shargleam Blackcap	Ch Halstock Primula of Ravenscrest	Mrs P. Lock
Ch Exclyst Moonshine	23 May 1980	Ch Damases Tarquol of Ryshot	Ch Elizabeth of Exclyst	Mrs Brenda Philips
Sh Ch Wolfhill Dolly Parton	20 April 1980	Ch Wizardwood Teal	Halstock Leonora	Mr & Mrs J. S. Morgan
Sh Ch Withybed Country Maid of Shargleam	5 September 1980	Ch Tonggreen Squall	Ch Shargleam Black Abby of Withybed	Mr & Mrs R. Adams
Sh Ch Shargleam Turtle Dove of Fossdyke	1 December 1980	Oakmoss Woodpecker of Shogun	Shargleam Bunting	Miss P. Chapman
Ch Shargleam Water Pippit	1 December 1980	Oakmoss Woodpecker of Shogun	Shargleam Bunting	Miss P. Chapman
Ch Branchalwood Whinyeon	25 April 1981	Ch & Ir Ch Shargleam Blackcap	Ch Branchalwood Frisa	Mr & Mrs Dalziel & Mrs M. Scott
Sh Ch Amellia Astral	30 January 1982	Ch & Ir Ch Shargleam Blackcap	Torwood Treasure Trove	Mrs C. A. Massey
Ch Rase Iona of Fossdyke	22 May 1982	Norton Royal & Regal	Rase Lapwing	Mrs Paddy Petch
Sh Ch Shargleam Willow Wren	23 March 1983	Ch & Ir Ch Shargleam Blackcap	Sh Ch Withybed Country Maid of Shargleam	Miss P. Chapman
Ch Riversflight Bobbin	21 June 1984	Glydesdown Kingsfisher	Ch Torwood Poppet	Mrs J. Griffiths
Sh Ch Wolfhill George Elliott	11 March 1985	Wolfhill Paddywhack	Halstock Leonora	Mrs J. Morgan

BRITISH-BRED FOREIGN CHAMPIONS

Dog or Bitch	Date of Birth	Sire	Dam	Breeder
Australia				
Aust Ch Stonemeade Shandygaff	6 August 1971	Hallbent Woodcock	Hallbent Dusk	P. Whittaker
Aust Ch Stonemeade Fine Lace	5 November 1973	Stolford Indelible	Stonemeade Fascination	P. Whittaker
Aust & NZ Ch Torwood Pacific Pea	9 August 1983	Torwood Percil	Torwood Dazzler	Mr & Mrs N. Jury
Aust Ch Roglans Night Raider	26 July 1984	Ch & Ir Ch Shargleam Blackcap	Ewlands Yuletide of Roglans	Mr & Mrs M. Roe
Belgium				
Int & Bel Ch Branchalwood Islay French FT Ch	18 February 1985	Ch Stantilaine Rory of Branchalwood	Ch Branchalwood Frisa	Mr & Mrs S. Dalziel & Mrs Scot
Canada				
Can & Am Ch Parkburn Brandy Boy	14 April 1969	Lysander of Tamara	Leah of Tamara	Mrs M. Jewell
Can Ch Creekside Bubbles	5 November 1971	Berriman Beall	Collyers Maybelle	Capt A. B. Downing
Can Ch Cleevemoor Black Rodney	10 May 1972	Wyndhamian Christopher of Exclyst	Claverdon Gossamer	C. Norris
Can Ch Branchalwood Feochan	25 August 1977	Tonggreen Squall	Branchalwood Maree	Mr & Mrs S. Dalziel
Can & Am Ch Heronsflight Burnet	16 March 1984	Ch Heronsflight Pan's Promise	Heronsflight Bryony	Mrs J. Mason

BRITISH-BRED FOREIGN CHAMPIONS

Dog or Bitch	Date of Birth	Sire	Dam	Breeder
Denmark				
Dan Ch Halstock Druid	6 February 1966	Collyers Blakeholme Brewster	Halstock Black Donna	Mrs P. Lock
Dan Ch Halstock Hunter's Moon	6 February 1969	Halstock Hamlet	Halstock Juanita	Mrs P. Lock
Int Chs & Dan Chs Woodwind and Woodworker	27 April 1969	Ch Tonggreen Sparrow Boy	Ch Woodpoppy	Colin Wells
Dan Ch Gelhams Zulu	29 June 1973	Ch Woodway Kenstaff Whipster	Collyers Maribu	Mrs Buxton
Int Ch & Dan Ch Downstream Forester	10 July 1973		Downstream Charm of Roysia	Mr & Mrs P. Johnson
Dan Ch Woodland Way	23 February 1975	Kenstaff Whipster Fenhunter Jack	Halstock Miranda	Paul Way
Int Ch & Dan Ch Westering Warcry	6 November 1975		Claverdon Fidelity	Mrs J. Smith
Dan Ch Black Magnus of Exclyst	3 September 1976	Ch Exclyst Bernard	Cleevemoor Black Coffee	Mrs J. Cornish
Int Ch & Dan Ch Belsud Black Falcon	8 April 1977	Apollo of Belsud	Belsud Hummingbird	Mrs M. Grimes
Finland				
Finn Ch Exclyst Noble Lad	15 October 1981	Wizardwood Sea Bird of Exclyst	Ch Midnight Star of Exclyst	Mrs B. Phillips
Germany				
German, Lux & Dutch Ch Heronsflight Trust	21 March 1969	Teal of Hawks Nest	Ch Heronsflight Black Bell of Yarlaw	Mrs J. Mason

Int Ch & Ger Ch Rase Tradmist	2 December 1972	Ch Wizardwood Sandpiper	Ch Rase Rumaigne	Mrs Paddy Petch
Ger Ch Brackenwood Winsome	21 July 1977	Leahador Wanderer of Tonggreen	Tormik Ash	Mr & Mrs D. Les
Ger Ch Vbos Veto	15 July 1978	Sh Ch Nortonwood Black Bart	Sh Ch Vbos Velma	Miss V. Ogilvy Shepherd W. Galloway
Ger Ch Bonnie of Candidacasa	30 December 1978	Sh Ch Nortonwood Black Bart	Sh Ch Vbos Vogue	
Ger Ch Heronsflight Pan's Pearl	18 April 1982	Glenwherry Oak	Heronsflight Pansy	Mrs J. Mason & Mrs R. Talbot

Italy

Int Ch & Ital Ch Donovan	22 April 1965	Ch Woodlark	Halstock Delia	Colin Wells
World Int & It Ch Rase Harlequin	17 December 1982	Kenstaff Mulberry of Heronsflight	Rase Kittiwake	Mrs Paddy Petch

Luxembourg

Lux & Dutch Ch Heronsflight Jinx	1 August 1972	Ch Wizardwood Sandpiper	Heronsflight Tassel	Mrs J. Mason

Netherlands

Dutch Ch Claverdon Duchess	24 December 1958	Bob of Riverglade	Claverdon Pavlova	Dr N. Laughton
Dutch Ch Black Cindy of Yarlaw	21 March 1967	Hartshorn Samphire	Black Lass of Yarlaw	Mrs R. Hutton
Dutch Ch Tonggreen Spray	29 March 1974	Tonggreen Starling	Ch Leahador Dusk of Tonggreen	Miss J. Chester-Perks
Dutch Ch Tonggreen Sprig	29 March 1974	Tonggreen Starling	Ch Leahador Dusk of Tonggreen	Miss J. Chester-Perks
Dutch Ch Heronsflight Pan's Pledge	18 April 1982	Glenwherry Oak	Heronsflight Pansy	Mrs J. Mason

BRITISH-BRED FOREIGN CHAMPIONS

Dog or Bitch	Date of Birth	Sire	Dam	Breeder
New Zealand				
NZ Ch Blackberry of Vanrose	6 June 1972	Stolford Sceptre	Halstock Saltens Sally	J. F. Davenport
NZ Ch Stolford Kings Ransom	13 December 1972	Ch Bordercot Stolford Doonigan	Ch Stolford Mrs Mopp	Mrs P. Robertson
NZ Ch Heronsflight Tipster	11 June 1976	Heronsflight Tercel	Fenrivers Lily	Mrs J. Mason
Norway				
Nor Ch Halstock Lone Ranger	4 March 1971	Halstock Downstream Daniel	Halstock Jade	Mrs P. Lock
Nor Ch Heronsflight Merry	1 April 1971	Ch Courtbeck Mercury	Ch Heronsflight Blackbell	Mrs J. Mason
Int & Nor Ch Celebrity of Ryshot	17 May 1973	Wyndhamian Christopher of Exclyst	Shirelf of Ryshot	Mrs J. Durman
Nor Ch Wizardwood Waxwing	2 June 1973	Wizardwood Sandpiper	Wyndhamian Christina	Mr & Mrs P. Forster
Nor Ch Rase Pierrot	7 April 1974	Ch Bordercot Stolford Doonigan	Ch Rase Rumaigne	Mrs Paddy Petch
Nor Ch Rase Patricia	7 April 1974	Ch Bordercot Stolford Doonigan	Ch Rase Rumaigne	Mrs Paddy Petch
Nor Ch Hallbent Dawn Patrol	31 July 1974	Yonday Marshall	Hallbent Dark Dawn	Miss G. Buchanan
Nor Ch Algrous Ambrose	28 August 1974	Yonday Marshall	Hallbent Linnet (sent out in whelp)	Mr Algrov
Nor Ch Exclyst Iceman	12 October 1978	Ch Belsud Black Buzzard	Ch Elizabeth of Exclyst	Mrs B. Phillips
Nor Ch Exclyst Kestrel	22 May 1979	Tonggreen Sweat Pea	Ch Elizabeth of Exclyst	Mrs B. Phillips

Nor Ch Torwood Plague Nor Ch Shargleam Falcon	17 June 1979 6 September 1981	Torwood Percil Oakmoss Woodpecker of Shogun	Torwood Dazzler Shargleam Bunting	Mr & Mrs N. Jury Miss P. Chapman

Portugal

Port Ch Rase Kaffir	23 October 1980	Kenjo Black Knight	Rase Nutmeg	Mrs Paddy Petch

South Africa

SA Ch Halstock Enterprise	4 April 1968	Downstream Daniel	Halstock Joanna	Mrs P. Lock
SA Ch Stolford Nicholas of High Stakes	24 December 1972	Ch Woodway	Ch Stolford Wychmere Black Seal	Mrs P. Robertson
SA Ch Nortonwood Ebony Beau	31 January 1977	Yonday Marshall	Stolford Chanelle	Mr & Mrs R. Bradbury
SA Ch Shargleam Black Lace	26 June 1977	Ch Damases Tarquol of Ryshot	Ch Yonday Willow Warbler of Shargleam	Miss P. Chapman
SA Ch Exclyst Kismet of Redsteps	22 May 1979	Tonggreen Sweet Pea	Ch Elizabeth of Exclyst	Mrs B. Phillips

Sweden

Int & Swed Ch Downstream Hestia	1 November 1963	Winkswood	Downstream Pax	Mrs S. Johnson
Swed Ch Claverdon Fantasia	14 April 1967	Teal of Hawks Nest	Claverdon Rhapsody	Dr N. Laughton
Swed Ch Crikey of Heronsflight	16 July 1972	Ch Fenrivers Golden Rod	Heronsflight Rungles Jancy	Mrs M. Williams
Swed Ch Heronsflight Jade	1 August 1972	Ch Wizardwood Sandpiper	Heronsflight Tassel	Mrs J. Mason
Swed Ch Blakeholme Jamie	17 October 1972	Windgather Dirk	Ch Blakeholme Just So	Miss C. B. Hall
Swed Ch O'Flanagan Rule Britannia	1983	Kenstaff Mulberry of Heronsflight	Exclyst Morning Mist (sent out in whelp)	Mrs Lena Hagland (Mrs B. Phillips)

BRITISH-BRED FOREIGN CHAMPIONS

USA

Dog or Bitch	Date of Birth	Sire	Dam	Breeder
Am Ch Halstock Javelin	11 November 1961	Pewcroft Perch	Sh Ch Halstock Black Jewel	Mrs P. Lock
Am Ch Halstock Echo	4 April 1968	Downstream Daniel	Halstock Joanna	Mrs P. Lock
Am Ch Blakeholme Heronsflight Try	21 March 1969	Teal of Hawksnest	Ch Heronsflight Black Bell of Yarlaw	Mrs J. Mason
Am Ch Couallanby Remus	1 May 1969	Ch Fenrivers Golden Rod	Halstock Delia	Mrs D. P. Mathews
Am Chs Claverdon, Gamble and Gossamer	5 July 1969	Hartshorn Gaff	Claverdon Rhapsody	Dr N. Laughton
Am & Can Ch Yonday Swagman	1970	Ch Tonggreen Sparrow Boy	Claverdon Flapper	Flt Lt G. Snape
Am Ch Heronsflight Pertinance	31 March 1970	Heronsflight Tercel	Heronsflight Pert	Mrs J. Mason
Am Chs Wyndhamian Collector, Constructor and Cormorant	7 April 1971	Heronsflight Tercel	Woodlass	Mrs B. Phillips & E. Atkins
Am Ch Cracker of Heronsflight	16 July 1972	Ch Fenrivers Golden Rod	Heronsflight Rungles Jancy	Mrs M. Williams
Am Chs Wyndhamian Dare, Dash, Devil and Doll	12 October 1972	Forestholm Rufus	Woodlass	Mrs B. Phillips & E. Atkins
Am Ch Exclyst Druid	15 March 1975	Wizardwood Blackcap of Halstock	Exclyst Bright Shadow	Mrs B. Phillips
Am Ch Tonggreen Solomon's Seal	4 May 1976	Leahador Wanderer of Tonggreen	Tonggreen Sparrowgirl	Mrs P. Cowley

Am Ch Torwood Peerless CDEX WDEX	17 June 1979	Torwood Percil	Torwood Dazzler	Mr & Mrs N. Jury
Am Ch Torwood Poppy	17 June 1979	Torwood Percil	Torwood Dazzler	Mr & Mrs N. Jury
Am Ch Shargleam Black Woodpecker	1 December 1980	Oakmoss Woodpecker of Shogun	Shargleam Bunting	Miss P. Chapman
Am Ch Pendlewych Peregrine	27 September 1982	Tonggreen Storm Petrel	Ch Larg Linnet of Pendlewych	Mrs M. Ayre
Am Ch Black Jack	9 October 1983	Ch Bordercot Guy	Tokeida Midnight Mischief	A. Murray
Am Ch Shargleam Shorelark	17 October 1983	Ch Withybed Country Lad	Ch Tonggreen Swift Lark of Tonggreen	Miss P. Chapman
Am & Can Ch Heronsflight Burnet	16 March 1984	Ch Heronsflight Pans Promise	Heronsflight Bryony	Mrs J. Mason
Am & Can Ch Branchalwood Ettrick	10 July 1984	Ch Stantilaine Rory of Branchalwood	Ch Palnure Pride of Branchalwood	Mr & Mrs S. Dalziel

WORKING CHAMPIONS

Dog or Bitch	Date of Birth	Sire	Dam	Breeder
Dual Ch Grouse of Riverside (dog)	1 March 1903	Ch Horton Rector	Luton Melody	Miss Grey
Dual Ch Toby of Riverside (dog)	4 May 1919	Punch of Riverside	Dart	Cmdr Ellison RN
FT Ch Elwy Mary (bitch)	7 May 1928	Ch Dandie of Shipton	Bibby	P. Barratt
FT Ch Windle Popular (bitch)	19 January 1931	Ch Specialist	Atherbram Biddy	W. J. Phizacklea
FT Ch Hartshorn Sorrel (bitch)	18 May 1962	Teal of Hawks Nest	Nesfield Stratton	Wilson Stephens
FT Ch Nesfield Michael (dog)	1965	Blakeholme Joiner	Hartshorn Midnight	Major Wilson
FT Ch Werrion Redwing of Collyers (bitch)	8 May 1973	Ch Wizardwood Sand-piper	Collyers Juno	Mrs J. Remington-Hobbs

11

Useful Information on the Breed

The demand for good specimens of the breed has led to many well known affix holders exporting dogs from England so that there are now Flat Coats in many countries in the world. Flat Coated Retriever Societies have been established in America, Canada and Holland, while Sweden, Denmark, Norway, Germany and some other countries belong to joint Retriever Clubs so that shows and field trials are run in conjunction with them.

America
The Flat Coated Retriever Club of America was founded in 1960 when Homer and Merc Downing imported Pewcroft Prefect and

1986 World and International Italian Ch Rase Harlequin (Floppy).
Bred by Paddy Petch, owned by Costanza Rimini Calabrese, Italy.

Atherbram Stella for the foundation of their Bramcroft Kennel. The Rabinda prefix of Ed and Dorothy Moroff came about from the mating of Rab of Morinda and Jet of Lilling while Sally Terroux bought Champion Claverdon Duchess and formed the basis for her Terrcroft Kennel, although these days her dogs carry the prefix of Montayo. Shortly after these three members formed the society in America they were joined by Ed Atkins, a doctor by profession, with Champion Halstock Javelin. The Club's membership in March 1978 was up to 210, widespread throughout the States where the interest was actively flourishing and to date now numbers over 500. There are three newsletters a year edited by Biz Reed from Minnesota and the present President of the Flat Coated Retriever Society is Valerie Bernhardt, who lives in Milford, Pa., both of whom are members of the English Flat Coated Retriever Society. There are both show and work interest catered for in the American Society and there are around eighty shows from which major points can be earned. The first working certificate was initiated in 1975 and the first Annual Speciality Show in March 1978. Field trials and Obedience qualifying Companion, Utility and tracking titles are also part of the Flat Coat scene in America.

Canada
The Flat Coated Retriever Society of Canada was started by Peter and Cyraine Dugdale when they went out to that country in 1974 in conjunction with Mr and Mrs Crawley and Mr and Mrs Doug Windsor from Ontario. Although the breed was quite strong in the 20s and 30s, the war did not help numbers, and the earlier kennels seem to have dissipated over that period leaving Canada with virtually no Flat Coats until a number of imports revived the breed after thirty years. The first Booster Show for Flat Coats (a Booster Show is where a Breed Club offers extra trophies to boost an entry at a particular Championship show) was held in Toronto in March 1975, six months after the Club's inauguration and attracted an entry of nineteen from as far away as Laramie, Wyoming and included Moira Jewell from Britsh Columbia. Moira had emigrated from England the previous year taking with her Parkburn Brandy Boy who was already an English Show Champion and who was to go on to win both his Canadian and American titles. The first Championship Show was held in 1976 when there were twenty-six entries, people travelling right across the country from east to west, which are vast distances in Canada by anyone's standards. Membership now stands at around twenty-five including a number of the American 'field people'. The Society's first Honorary Member was

the late Mr H. V. P. 'Bumpy' Lewis who had been interested in Flat Coats since the early 30s when he imported a number of Mr W. Skerry's Towerwood dogs from England. He was actively concerned as chairman of the Canadian National Sportsmen's Shows which run for ten days during March, consisting of seven dog shows, five obedience trials and daily invited competitors taking part in the evening indoor field trials along with all types of outdoor life exhibitions. The Secretary of the Canadian Club is Mrs Janet Levecque from Acton, Ontario. Flat Coats in Canada take part in all aspects of work and show proving they are indeed dual purpose.

The Netherlands

The Dutch Flat Coated Retriever Club was founded in September 1972 with fifty members by the late Mrs Carrie van Crevel (who started with a Yarlaw bitch, Cindy of Yarlaw) supported by Leonie Galdermans (who owns Dutch Champion Heronsflight Pan's Pledge), Mrs Borghorst and Mr Jaap Mulder (Claverdon Lofty). They now have a membership of around six hundred which is about all the Flat Coat owners in the country. The majority of home bred dogs in Holland are the progeny of Champion Black Cindy of Yarlaw though as can be gathered, Heronsflight, Claverdon and also Halstock stock

Flat Coats in Holland. (Photograph: David Dalton)

are in evidence, and odd Ryshot and Downstream dogs have also been exported in the early days. The Dutch are interested in keeping the dual purpose of the breed functioning and the Royal Dutch Shooting Club organises working tests in different parts of the Netherlands having upwards of eighty dogs competing (though not all Flat Coats, of course!). The Flat Coated Retriever Club also organises several working tests of varying standards of ability through the season on their own plus a yearly beauty show. They lay down very strict rules about membership of the Club and the present official is Mrs Rathenau Beyerman from St Michielsgestel, who is now the Secretary. All the members of the Dutch Club mentioned here are also members of our own Society in England. The previous Secretary, Mrs Rueb, is now living in England.

Norway
Although there is not a Flat Coated Club in Norway itself there is a strong interest in the breed. There are several imported Flat Coats that have been made up to Champion: Champion Hallbent Dawn Patrol, still going strong at eleven years old, Champion Rase Pierrot, Champion Rase Patricia, Champion Blakeholme Jamie, Champions

Mrs B. Halldis Flakin's Norwegian Champion Hallbent Dawn Patrol, sire of 14 Norwegian champions (DOB 30.7.74). Bred by Georgie Buchanan.

Norwegian champions Skogstad's sigma (right) and Gledill Algera (left).

Exclyst Iceman and Kestrel and Champion Downstream Hestia (who lived to be seventeen and a half years of age) to name a few, and the man who looks after the breed interests in Norway is Per Iversen who lives near Oslo. He is also a member of the English Society and visits shows over here several times a year.

Sweden
The Flat Coated breed in Sweden is affiliated to the Swedish Spaniel/Retriever Club and has a membership of around six hundred taking in Flat Coat owners from Finland, Denmark, Norway and Germany. The prime mover of the work for the breed is done by Stig Olsson from Rimfors who also belongs to our Society and he is concerned with the publication three times a year of a booklet on news and views of the breed called *The Charmer*. Both aspects of the breed are cultivated strongly.

Denmark
The Danish Retriever Club caters for the breed in this country. There is much interest in both work and show and the man to whom

correspondence should be addressed is also a member of the English
Club, Mr Poul Rønnow Kjeldsen of Rønde. There are about four
hundred Flat Coats in the country now. Many well known English
kennels have exported to Denmark.

Finland

There are about a hundred Flat Coats in Finland, some of them
being imported from Sweden, which forms the basis for Finnish
stock, the second generation of which was born in 1975. Between
two to four litters are bred a year and these owners belong to the
British Retriever Club. Most Flat Coats are kept in Finland as pets
and show dogs but an increasing number of people are also showing
now. Blakeholme, Halstock, Ryshot and Downstream are the basic
English kennels represented.

Germany

There are about one hundred and forty Flat Coats registered under
the auspices of the German Retriever Club at the present time. I
actually exported the first Flat Coat to Germany after the war in 1973
in Rase Tradmist but it was not until six years later there was the
interest to start the breed properly and the first all-German litter was
bred in 1980. Secretary of the German Retriever Club is Brigitte
Schneidermann of Krefeld, who has Flat Coats herself.

New Zealand

At the last count the Flat Coat population in New Zealand totalled
around one hundred and fifty. The first import was New Zealand
Champion Stolford Kings Ransom who lived to be fifteen and only
died recently, while the oldest home bred Flat Coat is Champion
Vanrose Black Cindy who is now eleven. There are between forty
and fifty members who do their best to show and work with what is
very definitely a minority breed. The Secretary is Carol Jorgensen
(Voyager kennel) in Levin.

Australia

Flat Coats have been going longer in Australia than in New Zealand
and consequently several have been exported to the latter country to
help them get going. The first import from England was from Philip
Whittaker's kennel and eventually became Australian Champion
Stonemeade Shandygaff. There is a Victorian Flat Coat Association
covering New South Wales, Queensland and South Australia. The
Secretary is Peter Ely of Werribee, Victoria, and the President, Kim
Methven, of Gembrook, Victoria. Membership numbers about forty.

Assia Vom Timmermor owned and bred by Karla and Werner Mayer in Germany. Sired by the first English export Rase Tradmist.

South Africa
The advent of Flat Coats in South Africa is very recent as in 1970 Mrs Gay Gamley went out to Rhodesia taking with her Halstock Huntress and Halstock Enterprise. Under the prefix Dabulamanzi (Zulu for cleaving or attaching to water) several litters were bred before returning to England in 1976. Three years earlier Miss Adele Newmarch (of Highstakes affix) imported Stolford Nicholas from Peggy Robertson. He soon got his title and was used on bitches bred by Gay Gamley and brought in as Highstakes foundation brood bitches by Miss Newmarch. Nicholas was mated to Dabulamanzi Bembazana of Highstakes. This mating produced Champion High Stakes Ripple (who had several placings in Novice Field Trials), Champion High Stakes Amazing Grace and Champion High Stakes Searcher of Kilifi, a multiple show winner.

In 1977 Miss Newmarch brought in Nortonwood Ebony Beau from the Bradburys and two years later used him on Dabulamanzi Bembazana, producing three champions, High Stakes Digger, Dasher and Dinah. He has been used successfully several times since. At the end of the same year a Mr McGladdery in Rhodesia brought over Tonggreen Sparrowgrass at the age of eighteen months from English breeders Cowley and Perks. He bought Dabulamanzi Chinyika from Gay Gamley and had one or two litters when he moved to South Africa from Rhodesia.

Early in 1978 Gail Cook imported Shargleam Black Lace of Wayyikria (sister to Blackcap) who produced a litter of twelve to Ebony Beau from which came Champions Wayyikra Broque, Bracken of Klynroc, Braid and Brett, all proving to be dual purpose. Black Lace changed hands to Miss Newmarch in 1982 gaining her title en route.

Peter and Christine Sandford emigrated to South Africa from the United Kingdom plus Exclyst Kismet of Redsteps who also became a Champion and Top winning South African bitch in 1982. About a year later, the Greens also emigrated plus Heronsflight Justice and his liver son, Bantu's Boy, who, when put to Redsteps Emily, produced two liver puppies, the first to be born in South Africa. The latest import is Bishopmanor Bilberry of Rothsay, a Blackcap son brought over by the Davisons and he has just sired his first litter, but there are on average only about two litters a year bred in South Africa.

ENGLISH KENNELS
We have several stalwarts of the breed that started their kennels after the Second World War and have been in the Society since the early days. I haven't space to mention them all but I thought you might

find a few potted biographies interesting so if we start with the Patron:

Dr Nancy Laughton MD DPH author of *A Review of the Flat Coated Retriever* published in 1968, has kept and bred flat coats mostly on the working side for over thirty years, choosing Champion Claverdon Jet as a foundation bitch in 1944 and the dog Revival of Ettington from W. J. Sims about the same time. The result of this mating was a bitch, Claverdon Faith, who was herself mated to Champion Waterman and their progeny included the two champion dogs Waterboy and Workman and the bitches Champion Watchful and Champion Claverdon Black Velvet who went to Miss Meeson to restart her Rettendon strain. Another bitch from this litter, Claverdon Celeste, produced Champion Claverdon Miss Tinker when mated to Champion Atherbram Nobbie and she was the foundation bitch for Major Wilson's Nesfield kennel in Ireland, while a fourth bitch was Champion Black Satin, thus making six champions out of the one litter which surely must be near a record. Dr Laughton tended to try and use the old working lines of Bryn Asaph, Sauch and Atherbram, keeping the best of each litter to carry on the line. She was the first Secretary of the newly formed Flat Coated Retriever Society in 1948.

This Society now has four Vice Presidents of which the first is **Brigadier F. W. Clowes** who retired from the Presidency in 1977 after twenty-one years. A keen shooting man and popular field trial judge, obtaining his first Flat Coat in 1912, Brigadier Clowes had no chance till hostilities ceased to indulge in his hobby but soon after this he bought Hark of Lingwood (of Atherbram breeding) and Breeze of Lingwood (part Bryn Asaph, part Adlington) to found his Lingwood prefix. He has now given up breeding and has bought in Yarlaw and Blakeholme dogs to assist with his shooting.

Second of the Vice Presidents is **Colin Wells** who is, I think, the oldest pre-war survivor to be still breeding continuously, although now through his son, having had a break for service in His Majesty's Forces in the Second World War. This kennel does not actually have a prefix though all the dogs are named with the letter 'W'. Colin Wells who for years was the Head Keeper to the Duke of Rutland has now retired, and has therefore more time to devote to his own dogs' training, for this is one of the most successful of the working kennels, but it is by no means one-sided for Colin has had more than his fair share of wins in the show ring too. Originally founded in 1933 with a bitch bought from Adam Gordon called Salthill Special (Champion Specialist ex Kirkhill Tib), she was bred to a dog called Buzzard, also sired by Specialist, and one of the bitch puppies named Miss Celeste was the dam of Revival of Ettingdon who could trace her male pedigree back to the Leecroft dogs of Ellis Ashton. After the war, in 1945 Colin bought in Claverdon Faith, a bitch out of Revival and an Atherbram dog he called Waterman, who won twelve Challenge Certificates and was Best of Breed at Crufts four times, as well as running well in trials. The resultant mating of these two produced the Champions Waterboy and Workman. For nine years running Waterman and Workman (his son) shared Best of Breed at Crufts with the latter just beating his father five to four in a successive run. They both worked well in trials, Champion Waterboy gaining twelve awards in thirteen runs but just failing to make his dual title in the mid fifties. About the same time two Claverdon bitches were imported into the 'W' kennel, these being Waternymph and Tawny Pippet, both of whom also became champions and field trial winners. Tawny Pippet's most famous son was champion Woodlark (by Champion Waterboy) and daughter, Champion Wave (by Champion Workman), who in her turn produced Champion Waveman (by Blakeholme Jem). Two pick of litters from Colin's Champion Woodlark brought into the 'W' kennel Champion Donovan and Champion Woodpoppy (to which much of my own Rase line harks back), the dog later being sold abroad and becoming an International Champion. Another Champion was Woodman who was exported to Sweden at a later date. To the best of my reckoning in the last thirty years Colin Wells has produced over twelve champions in the breed, all of them field trail award winners into the bargain. He has had a Best of Breed winner at Crufts at least fourteen times with successive runs of a four and a nine and there can't be a more obvious example of true dual purpose breeding in any gun dog breed let alone Flat Coats.

A member of many years' standing was the third Vice President, the late **Miss C. B. Hall** and her 'Blakeholme' breeding. Although she obtained her first Flat Coat in 1922 (that was Hawkesmore Ben) she did not start breeding until after the Second World War when she bought Pewcroft Prim born in 1953 by Denmere Prince ex Champion Pewcroft Pitch which she mated to both Champion Waterboy and Champion Waterman and the resulting progeny produced a number of champions both here and in Sweden. Rettendon Spoonbill was acquired in 1961 and mated to a dog of the above breeding, Blakeholme Jem, who had previously sired Champion Collyers Blakeholme Brewster, Champion Stolford Whinchat and Champion Waveman. Two of the daughters from Spoonbill and Jem were in time bred to Champion Fenrivers Golden Rod and many of the progeny worked well in field trials, thus endorsing Miss Hall's

Working Trial duo. Mrs Rita Aubrey and Blakeholme Jet CDEx, UDEx, WDEx, TDEx. (Photograph: David Dalton)

aim to produce dual purpose dogs stressing both temperament and character.

The Honourable Mrs Amelia Jessel, fourth Vice President, was Secretary of the Flat Coated Society for twenty-five years and she followed that by a term as Field Trial Secretary. She had been accociated with the breed for five years prior to that date with the purchase of the bitch Champion Asperula who worked for her husband. Asperula had three litters, the first by Ryshot Rungles Trademark was in 1958 and subsequently she was mated to Mrs Jessel's other two dogs, Claverdon Skipper and Champion Collyers Blakeholme Brewster producing stock which was truly dual purpose.

The present President of the Society is **Mr Reed Flowers** who farms and shoots in Norfolk. His Fenrivers kennel came into the limelight in 1953 with the purchase of the bitch Champion Pewcroft

Proper (Denmere Prince ex Champion Pewcroft Pitch). She was mated to Champion Waterboy two years later, Reed keeping a bitch Alyssum at home to work in trials, and selling Asperula who became the first champion for the Collyers kennel of which she was the foundation bitch. A dog from the same litter, Adonis, also gained his title. Champion Pewcroft Proper also had litters by Champion Workman and Champion Atherbram Pedro. It was her daughter Alyssum when bred to Pedro (Nobby of Riverside ex Atherbram Rosebud) who produced the bitch, Fenrivers Evergreen, dam of this kennel's most famous dog to date, Champion Fenrivers Golden Rod who, though now dead, won Best of Breed at Crufts for two years running in 1967 and 1968 and took thirteen Challenge Certificates plus field trials awards. (His litter sister was Fenrivers Erica, an early bitch for the Downstream kennel.) This dog was in direct male line of descent through Jimmy of Riverside to those early champions High Legh Blarney and Darenth.

A past President is **Mr Wilson Stephens**, one time editor of *The Field* and contributor to many country journals on the subject of gundogs. He and his wife started their Hartshorn kennels in 1958 with the bitch Nesfield Stratton who turned out to be a first rate worker. She was mated to Champion Woodlark and of the four resulting bitch puppies produced, two made it in the show ring – Show Champion Stolford Hartshorn Memory and Hartshorn Mudlark – and two won places in AV Open Field Trial Stakes while a bitch of a second mating (to Teal of Hawksnest) was sold to Major Wilson who produced International Field Trial Champion Hartshorn Sorrel to qualify in both Britain and Eire.

The **Johnsons, Peter and Shirley**, have been members of the Breed Society since the late fifties for him and the very early sixties for her, and they founded their kennel prefix Downstream in the same year as their marriage in 1963. Peter, who is a gamekeeper, started off with Winkswood (half brother to Champion Woodlark) while Shirley had acquired a black bitch, Ryshot Driad, through a chain of circumstances. The kennel foundation really started with the acquisition of Fenrivers Erica and another bitch, Wish, line bred to Champion Waterman, which was mated to Winkswood and produced Downstream Manto which was sold to another gamekeeper, Mr M. E. Darcy, and won several stakes for him. This is another kennel whose policy is to produce dual purpose dogs and both Downstream Hercules and International Champion Downstream Hestia (exported to Sweden) have done well in the show ring. Current contender for this kennel is their Downstream Vagabond. Shirley is a member of the Breed General Committee, Cup Steward and Litter Secretary, while Peter is at present the Field Trial Secretary.

Another member of the present committee and my breed note columnist writer for the rival paper *Our Dogs* is **Mrs Joan Mason** whose Heronsflight Flat Coat Retriever prefix was founded by the purchase of Black Bell of Yarlaw from Air Commodore Hutton and his wife's Yarlaw Kennels in 1964, though Joan had been in dogs with the prefix Ryton End since 1947 and with Heronsflight Goldens since 1954. Her first Flat Coat bitch was bought from the O'Neils' kennel and was called Heronsflight Pert. She was technically the last Pewcroft bitch that Stanley O'Neil bred and was by Pewcroft Proxy ex Pewcroft Putt. Heronsflight Black Bell of Yarlaw was mated to Teal of Hawksnest and from that litter emerged Leonie Galderman's German, Luxembourg and Dutch Champion Heronsflight Trust (which has had a great influence on the breed in Holland). American Champion Blakeholme Heronsflight Try, Heronsflight Tell, Herons-flight Tassel (who when mated to Champion Wizardwood Sandpiper produced the Luxembourg and Dutch Champion Heronsflight Jinx, again owned by Leonie Galdermans) and finally Heronsflight Tercil who sired a litter from Woodlass for Brenda Phillips out of which came American Champion Wyndhamiam Cormerant (who also won a Field Trial Award) and American Champion Wyndhamiam Con-structor. The well known working bitch Bruderkern Witch Hazel of Tarncourt was also sired by Tercil though the dam this time was Skeldyke Arla of Bruderkern, while New Zealand Champion Heronsflight Tipster was son to Tercil out of Fenrivers Lily.

In 1979 Joan was joined by her daughter, Rosemary Talbot, in a joint partnership under the Heronsflight prefix which produced the Pans litter of April 1982 giving Dutch Champion Heronsflight Pans Pledge (again owned by Leonie Galdermans) who was World Champion in 1985 and Reserve World Champion in 1986, German Champion Pans Pearl and English Champion Pans Promise. The latest in the long line of champions was Gillian Impey's American and Canadian Champion Heronsflight Burnet who was Best of Winners at Westminster in 1986 which is the American equivalent of our Crufts.

There are about twenty kennels that because of the dogs bearing their affix have become very well known names since the 60s, and although this also applies to one or two that have started since then, I haven't room to mention them all so I hope the reader will make allowances for the list presented for interest's sake.

Mrs Mary Grimes and Ch Belsud Black Buzzard winning a Pedigree Chum Champion Stakes Class with their representative who presented the award. (Photograph: David Dalton)

Belsud

In 1960 Peter Grimes presented to his wife Mary on the occasion of her birthday (she doesn't say which one!) a liver Flat Coat puppy bred by Mr F. M. McFarland called Brown Bella of White Rails (Ryshot Copper Ducket by Ryshot Copper Fern) to replace a mad Boxer who climbed curtains and ate boxes of fireworks and thus Sudie became the Grimes' foundation bitch of the Belsud kennels, the name coming from Bella and Sudie. Mary bought in Courtbeck Taurus from Helen Beckwith and made him up to champion and in addition has produced Champion Black Buzzard, Show Champion Magpie and Champion Brown Guillemot. Her latest dog, Capercaillie, has begun his quest for a title.

Bordercot

This kennel name has been well known for many years as Mrs Foreman, Rosalie Brady's mother, has been in Papillons from pre-war. In fact Rosalie took a Reserve Challenge Certificate with a Papillon bred by herself when she was only thirteen, following that with a Best of Breeds at Crufts aged seventeen. On the occasion of

Ch Bordercot Guy. Owned by Mrs R. Brady, winner of Dog CC, Best of Breed and Res in the Group at Crufts, 1985; Dog CC Crufts, 1986; Dog CC, Best of Breed and winner of Group Crufts, 1987. He is also a working dog. (Photograph: David Dalton)

Ch Bordercot Stolford Doonigan carrying a hare.
(Photograph: D. Pearce)

her marriage in 1967 she bought a Stolford dog for Gerald to shoot over and herself to show. Champion Bordercot Stolford Doonican filled both roles admirably, breaking the Breed Show record. Rosalie then obtained Stolford Mrs Mopp from Peggy Robertson and made her up three times over. At the age of nine Mopps took part in her first field trial winning a Certificate of Merit. Rosalie took possession of Bordercot Guy at the age of six weeks and eventually he too got his title. The present fore-runner is his daughter Beaver of Bordercot.

Branchalwood
This Scottish affix commenced its interest in Flat Coats in 1971 although Scott and Sheila Dalziel had had various breeds of gundogs spanning forty years up till then. Now joined by their daughter, Maureen Scott, Branchalwood dogs have gained thirty Challenge Certificates and twenty-four Reserve Challenge Certificates up to mid-1986. They started off with Glendaruel Catriona bred by Tom and Sally McComb and from her gained their first show dog, Branchalwood Maree, sired by Champion Wizardwood Sandpiper. They usually have one litter a year and have exported to a number of countries producing Canadian Champion Branchalwood Feochan. American and Canadian Champion Branchalwood Ettrick, and International French and Belgium Champion Branchalwood Islay, plus two Scottish home bred champions, Branchalwood Frisa and Whinyeon.

Bramatha
This kennel affix belongs to Sarah Whittaker for a long time involved with her father's Stonemeade kennel, then in the early 70s branching out on her own with Stonemeade Prince Charming who was mated to Stonemeade Atherbram Trollope. From this union Sarah kept Stonemeade Bertram in lieu of a stud fee. Miss Annabel Payne (great-niece of Will Phizackalea of Atherbram fame) was trying to find an Atherbram bred dog to mate to her bitch, Auriga of Hartmead at Atherbram, so she used Bertram. From this mating, Sarah kept the liver bitch, Atherbram Ability, who herself produced three litters. The first litter was to Norseman of Atherbram producing livers and blacks, one of the former, Bramatha Copper Nijinsky, went to Sweden. The second litter was to Downstream Nimble and the third to Falswift Black Storm but both only produced blacks. Bramatha Black Natasha from Ability's first litter was kept and mated to Champion Bordercot Guy producing Bramatha Copper Gunyah, and this bitch plus an adult bought in, Belsud Black Garganey, also carry the liver gene, so it is hoped to be able to go on breeding livers from black parents and so maintain good coat and eye colour in dual purpose dogs.

Casuarina

Peter and Cyraine Dugdale obtained a dog when they became resident in England in 1962 after many years of living abroad. They found they were next door neighbours to Captain Downing and his wife, who eventually had a litter of Flat Coats and so Creekside Bubbles (called Sherpa) came into the Dugdales' life in 1971. Realising they now owned a working gundog they took the bitch to Dennis Izzard for training and registered the affix Casuarina which is a tree that grows in tropical places for Cryaine remembered the forty foot Christmas trees of her childhood. In 1974, Cyraine and Peter had to go to live in Canada for three years so they took Sherpa with them to Ontario and with Jean Crawley and Doug Winsor started a Canadian Breed Society in company with Moira Jewell who had gone out in 1973. Sherpa gained her title becoming the first Canadian Champion for forty years. They obtained a dog from Moira called Parkburn Dextensing. He was both shown and worked, eventually obtaining his Canadian and American titles plus a Companion Dog stake. He gained his third title on returning home. The eventual mating of Sherpa and Tensing produced the bitch Casuarina Nootka who also became a Canadian Champion owned by the Leveques.

On their return to England, Peter and Cyraine settled in Hampshire where their main emphasis is on working and producing dual purpose dogs. Cyraine was Secretary of the Society from 1982 to 1985.

Courtbeck

Miss Helen Beckwith bought a bitch from Mrs Lock in July 1964 and she eventually became Show Champion Halstock Joanna. Duly mated to Champion Claverdon Comet in 1967, she produced a litter of eleven puppies, three of which were to become champions themselves. These were Tonggreen Courtbeck Venus, Courtbeck Mercury and Belsud Courtbeck Taurus who all in their turn produced a champion. This is a small kennel which has only had seven litters but Courtbeck dogs have done well in work and show both at home and abroad.

Crackodawn

The loss of a Labrador in 1966 caused Sheila Godbolt to change her breed allegiance and purchase a Flat Coat dog puppy, Stolford Indelible, from Mrs Peggy Robertson. Bred from Champion Stolford Whinchat by Show Champion Hartshorn Memory, Prince won two Challenge Certificates but died before he got his third. In 1969 Sheila bought her foundation bitch, Downstream Crissa (Champion Woodman × Downstream Halstock Hussey) from the Johnsons and the following year got her prefix Crackodawn granted by the Kennel Club. Honey was eventually mated to Reed Flowers' Champion Tonggreen Sparrow Boy in 1971. Since that time there have only been five litters, for Sheila of necessity breeds when she herself requires stock and her aim is to produce a good working line of proven temperament.

Exclyst
This prefix was registered at the Kennel Club in 1967 a year after Brenda Phillips had purchased Collyers Albertine from the Hon. Mrs Amelia Jessel, the then Secretary of the Breed Society. In 1970 she joined forces with American Ed Atkins under his prefix of Wyndhamian, and Woodlass owned by him came to Brenda in the same year. Mated to Heronsflight Tercil in the spring of 1971 the Wyndhamian 'C' litter produced American Champions Constructor, Collector and Cormorant, the latter dog also winning a number of American Field Trial Awards. Wyndhamian Christopher of Exclyst stayed at home and sired a number of English champions such as Champion Halstock Primula of Ravenscrest, Champion Elizabeth of Exclyst JW, Champion Midnight Star of Exclyst and Champion Puhfuh Phineas Finn, Foreign Champions, International and Norwegian Champion Celebrity of Ryshot, Canadian Champion Cleevemoor Black Rodney and the Danish multiple ticket winner Lone Lady of Exclyst.

Woodlass was then mated to Forestholme Rufus again, producing in October 1972 a number of American Champions in the 'D' litter. These were Wyndhamian Dare, Dash, Devil and Doll. With the success of these two litters Woodlass had the honour of being American Top Sporting Brood Bitch for 1971 and 1972.

During the last decade, Brenda has relinquished her partnership with Ed Atkins and under her own affix produced a number of winning dogs on the bench and in the field, namely Exclyst Bernard JW, his daughter Bernadette and grandson Exclyst Timemaster, who won the 1986 Welks heat of the Spiller/*Dog World* Puppy Stakes, Champion Exclyst Imperial Mint, Norwegian Champions Exclyst Iceman and Kestrel and South African Champion Exclyst Kismet of Redsteps while Exclyst Morning Mist was sent to Sweden in whelp to Kenstaff Mulberry of Heronsflight, out of which came International and Nordic Champion O'Flanigan Rule Britannia. More recently a mating of Champion Midnight Star to Wizardwood Seabird produced the Finnish Champion Exclyst Noble Lad and

Swedish Challenge Certificate winner Northern Dancer. The aim is to obtain good-looking show and working stock.

Glendaruel

This Scottish prefix is actually taken from the name of a glen in Argyll and Tom and Sally McComb re-registered it in 1968. I say re-registered because it had been in the ownership of a Mr C. Wiggan until 1923 (also for Flat Coats) after which it had lapsed for forty years until taken up by the McCombs. They started off with a bitch from Dorothy Montgomery, Kilbucho Honeybee (Betty), who was a grand-daughter of Champion Waveman. She was mated to Jet of Waveman (a son of Champion Waveman). The two best known bitches from that litter were Glendaruel Christina who went to the Telfers and when mated to Kenstaff Whipster produced Champion Stainilaine Rory of Branchalwood belonging to the Dalziels, Champion Glendaruel Gumboots owned by Tom and Sally, and Glendaruel Catriona who went to be the Dalziels' original brood bitch. They mated her to Champion Wizardwood Sandpiper and from that union kept Branchalwood Maree who herself gained two Challenge Certificates and was dam of Champion Branchalwood Frisia.

In 1975 on the death of Jimmy Boyd, Monarch of Leurbost was left to the McCombs who campaigned 'Archie' to his title and collection of a number of Challenge Certificates as well as working him on the grouse moors regularly in company with Betty. She lived to be one of the oldest Flat Coats when she died aged fifteen plus. Litters are not bred too frequently but when they are the aim is to produce a typical Flat Coat with workability bred from established mature bloodlines.

Hallbent

Georgie Buchanan founded the Hallbent Flat Coats in 1962 when she bought a bitch puppy from the Stevens in Balfron, Scotland, so Strathendrick Dawn came down to Essex to join the Hallbent Cockers. Georgie reckons to keep around four Flat Coats breeding once a year on average and has produced four English Champions and a Norwegian Champion to date. Champion Hallbent Gipsy Lad who was sire of three champions including my own Champion Rase Rumaigne had nine Challenge Certificates and Best of Breed at Crufts to his credit. He was born in July 1968. A repeat mating eleven months later produced Show Champion Hallbent Teal and her litter. Her brother Woodcock just missed out on his title but sired Champion Hallbent New Novel who went to Philip Whitaker as his foundation bitch, and another bitch, Dark Dawn, who was the dam of Norwegian Champion Hallbent Dawn Patrol, himself the sire of fourteen Norwegian Champions. Yet a third bitch, Hallbent Contessa, went to Jean Green as her Damases Foundation bitch and was dam to three champions in her only litter. Teal's grandson was Show Champion Hallbent Kim who is still winning at present, in company with Hallbent Soft Music owned by Pamela Stanley whose Open Show Best of Breed wins total eleven to date. Hallbent is predominantly a show kennel producing many winning Flat Coats.

Marlcot

Trevor and Kath Pennington founded their kennel in 1969 when they bought Marlcot Nicks Badger and Marlcot Nicks Jade from Colin Wells to be the start of this dual purpose line. They breed the occasional litter. Out of their retained puppies one of the best known was Marlcot Nicks Otter who had a number of Field Trial and Working Test Awards. One of the present dogs, Marlcot Nicks Dolphin, has won awards both in the field and in the show ring, collecting over fifty First Prizes. He won the Society Drum Goblet for Best Junior Show Winner in 1980 and a couple of years later took the URC Hants area Calcot Trophy for the retriever with most points in show and work. Other Drum winners have been Vixen, Lynx and Beaver. The Penningtons' policy is to breed occasionally with emphasis on temperament and soundness in dogs showing equal work/show potential.

Rase

I started in the breed in 1965 with the choice of a dog puppy, Tomani Bittern, bred from Yarlaw and Halstock lines. I had no other idea than just having a Flat Coat for myself to show and my husband to work but one or two successes tend to drive one on to become hooked. This is what happened to us and nothing would do but we buy a suitable mate for Jet and hope to produce a litter. In due time we acquired our brood bitch, Woodwren (Sweep) from Colin Wells and it is from her that my present stock can trace their pedigrees back in direct line.

I registered my affix in 1968 and duly produced the first Rase litter at the end of the following year keeping a dog and a bitch, Sambo and Susannah. Sam was used a few times at stud but Susie proved not to be able to breed so out of the litter Sweep had to Champion Hallbent Gipsy Lad I kept a further dog and bitch, Rase Romulus and Rumaigne (Pandy) both of whom were made up, Pandy winning awards also in the field. Her daughter Pipistrelle (by Champion Bordercot Stolford Doonican) also gained her title as did Champion Pierrot and Champion Patricia who were exported to

Norway from the same litter. Unfortunately, Pip too proved to be unable to be mated due to a 'restricted passage'. However, lines from both Pandy's daughters Lapwing and Nutmeg are now into the fifth generation as is the male Rase line originating with Sambo. Other foreign champions have been made up with International and German Champion Rase Tradmist, Portuguese Champion Rase Kaffir and Italian Champion Rase Harlequin, who was crowned World Champion in Vienna in 1986. The latest home-bred champion is Jill Saville's bitch Champion Rase Iona of Fossdyke.

Stonemeade

Philip Whittaker bought in Hallbent New Novel as a puppy from Georgie Buchanan in 1969. He later acquired her dam Hallbent Dusk, repeated the mating with Hallbent Woodcock and gave Stonemeade Prince Charming from that litter to his daughter, Sarah, to be the first dog in the Bramatha kennel. Dusk was mated to Champion Hallbent Gipsy Lad and out of those puppies Stonemeade Gipsy Bell remained at home where along with New Novel they gained working qualifiers, Novel going on to win her title. Dusk's final litter was again to Woodcock, and Stonemeade Shandy Gaff was exported to Australia as the foundation of the breed out there, where he gained his title.

New Novel was mated twice to Champion Wizardwood Teal, the first litter producing twelve black dogs. Black Emperor stayed at home but Stonemeade Duke and Huntsmann were exported to Denmark. From the repeat mating the Whittakers kept Jock and Constance. Black Emperor was mated to Shargleam Black Orchid and there were some yellow puppies in the litter so Emperor was given away to a pet home where he would not be used for breeding.

Philip bought in Atherbram Trollope as an adult bitch and mated her first to Champion Woodman, two of the resulting puppies being sent abroad, Wild Rose to Australia and Woodman to Denmark. Her second litter was to Stonemeade Prince Charming, and Sarah retained Stonemeade Bertram. He was in turn mated to Miss Annabel Payne's Auriga of Hartsmead which produced the liver bitch Atherbram Ability, who herself produced three litters with liver puppies in the first one only, to Norseman of Atherbram. Stonemeade is now trying to keep the liver strain active in both show and work puppies.

Tonggreen

Joan Chester-Perks started her Tonggreen retrievers in 1947 with labradors. She added Basenjis in 1951 and eight years later Flat

Coats. These were joined by Cavaliers, Cockers and the odd Golden before Pam and Terry Cowley took up a joint prefix with her in 1975. In the twenty-seven years of Flat Coat ownership there have only been twelve litters plus one Leahador bitch which Joan bred for Doreen Mitchell Innes producing Dusk and Wanderer.

The Tonggreen line was started with the purchase of Rettendon Linnet who was mated to Pewcroft Priam in 1962 from which Joan kept Swift and the Cowleys, Tonggreen Shrike. Tonggreen Swift was put to Fenrivers Golden Rod in 1966 and Linnet to Fenrivers Fern at the same time, producing between them fifteen dogs and two bitches, among them Champion Tonggreen Sparrow Boy which went to Reed Flowers and Tonggreen Starling who started off Judy Rolfe.

As Joan did not keep dogs and she had promised the only two bitches she had bred in the mid 60s she bought in Champion Tonggreen Courtbeck Venus who was one of the first to gain her Junior Warrant. At that time, 1966, there were only ten Championship Shows calssifying the breed and the Puppy and Junior Classes were mixed dog or bitch, but she still managed to collect thirty-eight points. In 1974 Champion Leahador Dusk of Tonggreen had a litter to Tonggreen Starling and produced Champion Tonggreen Squall and Dutch Champions Tonggreen Spray and Sprig before going to live with the Cowleys. American Champion Tonggreen Solomon's Seal was born in 1976 when Pam Cowley mated Leahador Wanderer to Tonggreen Sparrowgirl. Song Linnet was mated to Tomstan Hamlet in 1978 and Joan kept Song Siskin sending Stormbird to Denmark and Stormshrike to Germany. The mating was repeated in 1979 when Song Pippit went to the Cowleys and Storm Petrel to the Harkins. The only surviving pup of the Song Linnet × Leahador Wanderer litter in 1975 was Song Swift and she produced Champion Tonggreen Swift Lark of Shargleam. Tonggreen Swift Snipe, Swift Hawk and Swift Swallow, all exported to Germany. Their sire was Champion Shargleam Blackcap.

Over the years Champion Tonggreen Sparrowboy has sired six English Champions, two American Champions and three Norwegian Champions. His litter brother, Tonggreen Starling sired four English and two Dutch ones, while one of his sons, Tonggreen Squall, sired three Scottish Champions, the Adams' Withybed Country Lad and Maid and the Canadian Champion Branchalwood Feochan. The Harkins' Tonggreen Storm Petrel, *Our Dogs* Top Stud Dog in 1983 continues to keep the Tonggreen name to the fore.

Torwood
Denise and Neil Jury bought their first Flat Coat in 1967. This was

Ebony Reliance (Champion Waveman × Black Diamond) from Mr and Mrs T. Cooper of Weston on Trent and four years later joined the Flat Coat Society. In the same year, 1971, they registered their Torwood affix. Ebony Reliance was mated to Pegasus of Luda in January 1970 and again eighteen months later to Heronsflight Tercel from which litter they kept Torwood Trader for stud purposes. In 1975 Joan Mason gave them Heronsflight Puff as she was in and out of hospital and this bitch was used several times for breeding. The first time in the same year was to Windgather Dirk and produced Torwood Dazzler but the most noteworthy mating was to Herons-flight Tercel which produced Torwood Percel and champion Torwood Poppet which went as brood bitch to the Griffiths. In 1976 Joan had let the Jurys also have Heronsflight Twirl (by Tercel × Fenrivers Lily) who was shown fairly extensively. The litter in June 1979 of Torwood Percel × Torwood Dazzler produced Norwegian Champion Torwood Plague and American Champions Torwood Peerless CDEX WDEX and Torwood Poppy. A repeat mating in 1983 produced New Zealand and Australian Champion Torwood Pacific Pea. The other Torwood Champion was in 1981 when the union between Torwood Jolly and Bomore Traddles Girl of Torwood produced Champion Torwood Blue, the good working dog of Clive Harris. In the twenty years from 1967 twenty-eight Torwood litters have been bred.

Vbos
Velma Ogilvy Sheherd started with Cockers in 1935 with the original prefix of Oldfield but this eventually was taken by an English Setter kennel so Velma's father suggested she use the initials of her name and so Vbos came to be registered in 1946. She was interested in St Bernards and it was as a result of a twenty-five pence bet (five shillings in the old days) on Airborne in the Derby that netted her thirty-five pounds in winnings that she was able to buy her first one. But she had bad luck with them so when she met Jimmy Boyd and his Flat Coats decided she would change her breed. In 1966 Velma bought Vbos Stolford Inkspot (Stolford Whinchat × Show Champion Stolford Hartshorn Memory) and eventually mated her to Champion Tonggreen Sparrowboy, the union producing seven puppies, out of which she kept the bitch that eventually gained her title, Show Champion Vbos Velma. Put to Champion Stolford Bordercot Doonican, the mating produced Show Champions Vbos Vogue, Vbos Vanda, Vbos Vision and Vbos Viceroy. Her second litter was to Champion Nortonwood Black Bart which produced German Champion Vbos Veto, Champion Bordercot Guy and

Champion Black Velvet of Candidacasa at Waverton. Vbos Vanda was doing well until injured by a car, however Velma had also kept Vbos Vilne who was mated to Champion Falswift Apparition produced Vbos Video and Velmorn who was the dam of Vbos Victoria. Vogue's litter sister, Vanda, was mated to Champion Tonggreen Squall and produced Show Champion Nashville Dawn of Sedgedunum for the McCullums, and Vision mated to Bart was the dam of Vbos Velvetveen belonging to the Balls.

Velma only breeds once in three years when she is in need of stock replacement.

Wizardwood

Peter and Audrey Forster originally bred English Setters under their affix of Wizardwood, so named because of the legend in the Alderley Edge vicinity where they lived at the time. They joined the Flat Coat Society in 1969 when they acquired their first bitch, Windgather Delia, from Margaret Mothersill. She was mated several times, first to Champion Wizardwood Sandpiper in 1972, from which mating came Champion Wizardwood Wigeon. A repeat mating in 1974 produced Champion Wizardwood Teal and the following year she was put to the liver dog Fenrivers Ling and produced a mixed litter of livers and blacks, which included Wizardwood Tawny Owl, Show Champion Wizardwood Little Owl and Champion Wizardwood Brown Owl.

The same year as the Forsters bought Delia they acquired a second bitch, Halstock Jemimah, which they collected from deepest Dorset after the snowy Crufts of 1969. She was mated to Champion Tonggreen Sparrowboy in 1972 and the very well known dog Champion Wizardwood Sandpiper was one of these offspring, along with Wizardwood Turnstone that went to Mrs Rueb in Holland and Wizardwood Ruff who was sent out to Denmark and was never traced or paid for, with the result that Peter and Audrey made a conscious decision not to export any more dogs for at least ten years.

In 1970 Halstock Alicia, bred by Peggy Miller but owned by Patience Lock, joined the Wizardwoods and she eventually became a Show Champion. She was mated several times producing Wizardwood Black Grouse to Tawny Owl and Champion Wizardwood Hawfinch to Claverdon Jupiter.

Wyndhamian Christina bred by Brenda Phillips was also bought in about this time but she injured her leg at ten months which resulted in her having it amputated at seven. However, she lived happily on three legs until the age of fourteen. She was mated twice, the first litter to Sandpiper resulting in Norwegian Champion Wizardwood Waxwing in June 1973.

Champion Wizardwood Teal was a very useful worker who was borrowed on occasions by Peter Johnson who was working his own dog Woodway (litter brother to my Woodwren) or Robert as he was known, at the same time. One day when they had been working in water, Robert could not be found so Teal was sent to search for him and he found the dog hanging on to a branch in the water unable to get out, and he would certainly have died if left there much longer.

In order to keep the liver line, started with Tawny Owl, going forward the Forsters bought in the bitch Loversall Sutton in 1978 from Mr Dunston who had mated his bitch, Wizardwood Redwing, to Tawny Owl and their present successful young dog, Wizardwood Tawny Pheasant, is also by him. Their other youngster, Wizardwood Timber Wolf (Champion Shargleam Fieldfare × Show Champion Wizardwood Little Owl) is black and apart from winning his Junior Warrant was Top Flat Coat Puppy of 1983. The Forsters sent out to Denmark in 1986 Wizardwood Moonflower who is by Timber Wolf out of Wizardwood Tawny Kestrel. They hope to breed dual purpose work/show livers and blacks with a good eye colour.

Wolfhill

High up in the hills of mid Wales above Abermule in Powys stands a small farm, home of the Wolfhill Flat Coats. Stan and Jenny Morgan bought their first Flat Coat, Halstock Leonora, from Patience Lock in 1974, and she went on to win two Challenge Certificates but unfortunately missed out on the vital third one. She was mated to Champion Wizardwood Teal in 1977 out of which litter Wolfhill Hawthorn was kept and used sparingly at stud. Leonora had a second litter to Teal in 1980 which mating produced Champion Wolfhill Dolly Parton belonging to Valerie Livermore, and Wolfhill Box Car Willie who at present has one Challenge Certificate and a Reserve Challenge Certificate for the Jacksons.

The Morgans bought in a second bitch in 1975. This was Kempton Antigone of Wolfhill, bred by Mrs Ormsby from Champion Wizardwood Sandpiper × Champion Andromeda of Kempton, and to date she has won one Challenge Certificate and two Reserve Challenge Certificates. She was mated to Wolfhill Hawthorn in 1979 from which there were only two puppies, one going to Sweden while Wolfhill Paddywhack stayed at home. He was put to Leonora in 1985 and Show Champion Wolfhill George Elliott was one of the puppies from that mating. There have only been twenty-seven puppies bred in their eleven years in the breed and most Wolfhill dogs have been sold to working homes. This small kennel involves everybody in the family from father and mother to both daughters as chief exercisers (preferably behind the horses). They try to produce dual purpose type Flat Coats.

Yonday
George and Joan Snape set up the Yonday kennel in 1952 with Golden Retrievers. In 1963 they visited the 'Atherbrams' at Hill House near Tamworth and saw both liver and black Flat Coats, re-awakening memories for George of his father's two Flat Coats in the 1930s, one liver, one black, kept for rough shooting. When their last Golden died in 1968 they bought Claverdon Flapper (Teal of Hawks Nest × Cleverdon Rhapsody) from Dr Laughton. She gained two Challenge Certificates and three Reserve Challenge Certificates, also qualifying in the field. She was mated three times, first to Champion Courtbeck Mercury in 1971, which produced Yonday Marshall who collected seven Reserve Challenge Certificates and Show Champion Yonday Merry Maid. She was mated two years later to Champion Tonggreen Sparrow Boy which gave rise to American and Canadian Champion Yonday Swagman who went to Dorothy

One of the Wolfhill Flat Coats showing the horse how its done.

Snape's Yonday Marshal (Ch Courtbeck Mercury × Claverdon Flapper).

Moroff as a dual purpose dog in the USA. In 1974 she was mated to Woodland Whipster, this mating resulting in Champion Yonday Willow Warbler, the Shargleam foundation bitch for Pat Chapman. Her litter sister, Yonday Water Rail, was kept by the Snapes and mated to Tonggreen Storm Petrel producing Yonday Pandora, the present Yonday being campaigned with success.

Flapper's son Marshall was mated to Stolford Chanelle and sired litter brothers, Show Champion Nortonwood Black Bart and South African Champion Nortonwood Ebony Beau for the Bradburys in 1977, Norwegian Champion Hallbent Dawn Patrol out of Hallbent Dark Dawn in 1974 and Norwegian Champion Algrous Ambrose out of Hallent Linnet in the same year, while Black Bart is the sire of Champion Bordercot Guy and Champion Black Velvet of Candida-casa.

The following list of addresses I have found useful so I append them for your benefit.

Addresses
Animal Health Trust Small Animal Centre
Lanwades Park, Kennett, Near Newmarket, Suffolk

Canine Studies Institute
London Road, Bracknell, Berks RG12 6QN

Dog Breeders Insurance Co. Ltd
Beacon House, Lansdowne, Bournemouth, Hants.

Dog Breeders Associates
1 Abbey Road, Bourne End, Bucks SL8 4NZ

Pedigree Petfoods Education Centre
Waltham-on-the-Wolds, Leicestershire LE14 4RS

Pet Plan Ltd
319–327 Chiswick High Road, London W4 4BR

Pro Dogs
Rocky Bank, 4 New Road, Ditton, Kent ME20 4AD

National Canine Defence League
10 Seymour Street, Portman Square, London W1H 5WB

Peoples Dispensary for Sick Animals
PDSA House, South Street, Dorking, Surrey

Royal Society for the Prevention of Cruelty to Animals
The Manor House, Horsham, Sussex

The Kennel Club
1 Clarges Street, Piccadilly, London W1Y 8AB

For Export or Import of Dogs
Ministry of Agriculture, Fisheries & Food
Hook Rise South, Tolworth, Surbiton, Surrey

The history of the Flat Coated Retriever Society began in 1948 when there was an amalgamation of the Flat Coated Retriever Association with the Flat Coated Retriever Club producing the Flat Coated Retriever Society. The former Association had been very much work orientated and was founded by a number of well known shooting men of the time (1923) with the first field trial being held a year later. Although the Flat Coated Association did recognise the showing element, their Committee was criticised because it was said not enough was being done for the show side whose finances were in debit as a result. So a number of keen supporters of Mrs Murray Glover, who wanted to encourage a truly dual purpose dog, left the Association and formed the Flat Coated Retriever Club in 1937 which did very good work in encouraging the showing of Flat Coats in the period up to the outbreak of the Second World War in September 1939. This event effectively stopped activities in both clubs for the duration.

It was not until seven years later in 1947 that the Flat Coated Retriever Association under the presidency of Mr R. E. Birch recommended holding field trials, but it appeared to Mr Birch that Flat Coat ranks would be stronger it there was one voice instead of two, so with amalgamation in mind Mr Birch's committee and those of the Flat Coated Retriever Club met together in Chester in 1947. The result was the birth of the Flat Coated Retriever Society under a new President, Mr W. J. Phizacklea of the Atherbram prefix. The new body took over the cups and trophies formerly belonging to the Association on the understanding that field trials would still retain an important place in the Society's schedule. These are awarded as follows:

The Society Open Stake Field Trial

The Patrick Barratt Memorial Cup (given by the late Mr and Mrs
  Birch for best Gamekeeper's dog)
The Winch Cup (for the best Retriever)
The Oliver Challenge Cup (handled by a lady)
The Birch Challenge Cup (handled by an Amateur Owner)
St Hubert Challenge Cup (to highest Challenge Certificate winner)

The Birch Puppy Cup
The Olaf Trophy (the guns' choice)
The H. Hardy Memorial Trophy (Gamekeeper's/Owner/Member's
  award for dog best on a runner whether in awards or not)

The Society Any Variety – Non-Winners Stake

H. Hardy Memorial Trophy (as above)
Tarncourt Trophy (guns' choice)
The Yarlaw Trophy (Best Retriever)
The Collier's Trophy (Best Flat Coat)
Heather Trophy (for best Gamekeeper member in the awards)

For Winner of most Field Trial Awards in the Year

Riverside Challenge Cup (on a points scale)
Creton Cup (gamekeepers)

For Flat Coat gaining most points in both Field Trials and Shows

Pewcroft Memorial Trophy (also awarded on a points scale)

Winners at a Flat Coat Retriever Field Trial.
(Photograph: David Dalton)

On the show side the Society offers various cups and trophies to members annually, particularly at the United Retriever Club Championship Show held in August where the Stainton Challenge Bowl is on offer to best Post Graduate dog or bitch, the Allen Challenge Cup to the best Novice and the Atherbram Cup to best dog or bitch bred by the exhibitors. At the City of Birmingham Championship Show held the last weekend in August, Best of Breed wins the Claverdon Perpetual Challenge Cup. At the Flat Coat Championship Show usually held in April there are various trophies on offer:

Flat Coated Retriever Society Trophy for Best in Show
Fenrivers Trophy for Reserve Best in Show
Belsud Trophy for Best Opposite Sex
Rowland Tann Rose Bowl (Best Liver)
Downstream Trophy (Best Field Trial dog or bitch)
Ryshot Cup (Best Veteran)
Rase Trophy (Best Brace)
Larsson Trophy for Open Dog (Best Black Dog)
Courtbeck Trophy for Open Bitch
Heronsflight Trophy (Best runner Puppy, dog or bitch)

There is an Open show held at different venues all over the country at the end of September or beginning of October which has, besides the usual breed classification, two obedience classes with the winner being awarded the Sonbri Shield. Other cups and trophies for the sixteen dog and bitch classes are also awarded.

For the youngster winning the highest number of points during the year 1 January – 31 December in junior classes there is the Drum Goblet. Scoring wins at Open Shows count 3, 2 and 1 points for first to third placings and wins at championship Shows count 5, 4 and 3 points. The Becky Trophy is awarded to the dog gaining the most wins during the year.

Subscriptions to the Society are three pounds single, four pounds joint, Associates and Gamekeepers one pound fifty, OAPs one pound fifty and junior members seventy-five pence. These should be sent to the Hon. Treasurer, Miss Judy Rolfe, 7 Azalea Court, Floral Way, Andover, Hampshire SP10 3PS before 31 March, otherwise a rejoining fee of one pound is payable in addition to the subscription. A fee of one pound on joining is liable from new members. The Society is growing every year and at the time of writing numbers around 1,700 including about fifty junior members.

The '160' Club has a full membership with draws taking place every month and is almost a full time job for secretary Glenis Packham.

I ought to mention membership of the United Retriever Club also as Mr W. J. Phizacklea of the Atherbram prefix became its first Chairman on its inauguration at Birmingham in November 1946. The following year the United Retriever Club held its first show and in the same year, 1947, its first training class plus the very first working test ever held. The United Retriever Club now runs a Championship Show and two Open Shows in addition to three field trials yearly. The country is divided up into eight areas: Midland, Buckinghamshire, Border Counties and Cotswold, Essex, Hampshire and South West, Lincolnshire, North Midland and Southern, each running their own local training classes and working tests, taking it in turn to host the area working test final. Annual fees are single five pounds per annum, joint six pounds, Gamekeepers, juniors, etc one pound, payable on 1 October to the Secretary, Mr B. J. Hall, The Court House, Court Street, Sherston, Near Malmesbury, Wiltshire SN16 OLL. The Society produces a newsletter three times a year in January, June and October and the membership is around 1,300. Most Flat Coat owners also belong to the United Retriever Club in order to keep abreast with the working side of the breed and take part in the events in their areas.

I thought it might be quite interesting to list some of the well-established kennel names both past and present so here is the result in alphabetical order. Those marked * were in operation pre-war, that is prior to 1939.

A
*Adlington   Mrs Hemm
*Atherbram   Mr Phizacklea, on whose death the prefix was transferred to his niece, Mrs M. Payne, who dropped her previous prefix of Sharpethorne

B
Belsud   Mrs Mary Grimes
Bitcon   Mr Murray Armstrong
*Black   Major Harding Cox
*Blackdale   Mr Adam Gordon
Blakeholme   Miss C. B. Hall
Bordercot   Mrs Rosalie Brady
Brackernwood   Mr David Lees
Braemist   Mrs V. Jones
Braidwynn   Mrs H. K. Winton
Bramatha   Miss Sarah Whittaker

Bramcroft   Mr H. Downing
Branchalwood   Mr and Mrs Scott Dalziel and Mr and Mrs J. L. Scott
Bruderkern   Mr Bill Core
*Bryn Asaph   Mr R. E. Birch

C
Candidacasa   Miss E. M. C. Holmes
Casuarina   Mrs Cyraine Dugdale
Cedar Cottage   Mrs M. Camp
Claverdon   Dr Nancy Laughton
Cleevemore   Mr C. W. Norris
Clowbeck   Mr and Mrs R. Kitching
Collyers   The Hon Mrs Amelia Jessel
Coulallenby   Mrs Prim Matthews

Courtbeck   Miss Helen Beckwith
Crackodawn   Mrs Sheila Godbolt
Creekside   Captain A. B. Downing

D
Damases   Mrs Jean Green
*Danehurst   Mrs J. Inman
Darklens   Mr R. Allen
*Denmere   Mr Ken Barber
Downstream   Mr and Mrs Peter
   Johnson
Dudwell   Mrs C. Ross Thompson

E
Earlsworth   Mr and Mrs D. A. Earl
*Elwy   Mr P. Barrett
Emanon   Mr P. Miller
Eskmill   Mr and Mrs H. Donnelly
Everace   Mrs Eva Cook
Ewlands   Mr and Mrs W. Row-
   lands
Exclyst   Mrs Brenda Phillips

F
Fabiennes   Mrs Fay Thomas
Falswift   Mrs P. Westrop
Fenrivers   Mr Reed Flowers
Flowerdown   Miss Judy Rolfe
*Forestholm   Mrs P. M. Barwise
Fossdyke   Mrs J. Saville
Fredwell   Mrs J. Wells Meacham

G
Gelhams   Mrs Buxton
Glencooley   Mr Drew Gilpin
Glendaruel   Dr and Mrs Tom Mc-
   Comb
Glenridge   Mr and Mrs George
   Peacock
Glidesdown   Mr and Mrs Bill Gar-
   rod
Gowbarrow   Mrs D. Flint

H
Hallbent   Miss Georgie Buchanan
Halstock   Mrs Patience Lock
Hartshorn   Mr Wilson Stephens

Hasweth   Mrs P. Beard
Heronsflight   Mrs Joan Mason and
   Mrs Rosemary Talbot

I
Ikoshu   Mrs D. Horton

K
Kempton   Mrs Ormsby
Kenjo   Mr and Mrs K. Rudkin
Kilbucho   Mrs Dorothy Montgom-
   ery

L
Lacetrom   Mr and Mrs T. M. Gate
Leahador   Mrs Mitchell Innes
*Leecroft   Mr Ellis Ashton
*Leurbost   Mr Jimmy Boyd
Lindcoly   Mr and Mrs C. Saich
Linfern   Mrs J. McFadyen
Lingwood   Brigadier F. W. Clowes
Llecan   Mrs C. Fletcher
Luda   Mrs J. Pettifer

M
Maybrian   Mr and Mrs B. Pash
Marlcot Nicks   Mr and Mrs Trevor
   Pennington

N
Nantiderri   Mrs V. Rosser
*Nesfield   Major H. A. Wilson
Nethercrief   Mr and Mrs G. Smith
Nortonwood   Mr and Mrs Ron
   Bradbury

O
Oakmoss   Mr and Mrs George
   Lancaster

P
Paddiswood   Mrs N. Padley
Parkburn   Mrs Moira Jewell
*Pedders   Mr F. T. Allen
Pendlewych   Miss M. Ayre
Penmayne   Dr W. A. Reynard
*Pewcroft   Mr Stanley O'Neil

Piddlevalley   Mrs J. Kempe
*Pitchford   Colonel Cotes
*Ponsbourne   Mr E. W. Bryant
Puhfuh   Mrs Joan Shore
Pythingdean   Mr and Mrs P.
   Guthie

R
Rase   Mrs Paddy Petch
*Rettendon   Miss Meeson
Riversflight   Mr and Mrs P.
   Griffiths
*Riverside   Mr Reginald Cooke
Roglans   Mr and Mrs M. Roe
Rondix   The Hon Mrs R. Dixon
Rungles   Mrs G. Fletcher and Mr
   A. (Tinker) Davis
Ryshot   (Formerly) Margaret now
   Dennis Izzard under Bryshot Son
   Brian

S
Sandylands   Mrs Gwen Broadley
*Sauch   Mr S. S. Guy
Sedgeunum   Mr and Mrs A. Mac-
   Callum
Shargleam   Miss Pat Chapman
Sharland   Mrs Joyce Munday
Skateraw   Mrs M. M. Charles
*'Sp'   Mr W. Southam
Stantilaine   Mrs S. Telfer
Stolford   Mrs Peggy Robertson
*Stonehenge   The Reverend H.
   Walsh
Stonemeade   Mr Philip Whitaker
Strathendrick   Mr J. Steven

T
Tarncourt   Mrs Joan Marsden
Tomstan   Mr and Mrs Norman
   Stanley
Tonggreen   Mr and Mrs T. Cowley
   and Miss Joan Chester-Perks
Torwood   Mrs Denise Jury
*Tosca   Mr W. Simms
*Towerwood   Mr W. Skerry
Trewinnard   Mr W. J. Pascoe

V
Vbos   Miss Velma Ogilvy
   Shephard

W
Walford   Miss M. Walker
Warresmere   Dr Tim Woodgate
   Jones
Waverton   Mr and Mrs D. Hutch-
   ison
Westering   Mrs Janet Smith
Windgather   Miss Margaret
   Mothersill
Withybed   Mr and Mrs R. Adams
Wizardwood   Mr and Mrs Peter
   Forster
Woldsman   Miss M. Mawer
Wolfhill   Mr and Mrs J. Morgan
*Woodland   Mr Colin Wells now
   Wunderson Ron
Wyndhamian   Mr Ed Atkins and
   Mrs B. Phillips

Y
Yarlaw   Air Commodore and Mrs
   W. E. Hutton
Yonday   Flt Lt George Snape

Irish Champion and Champion Shargleam Blackcap

Before closing this chapter on bits and pieces of information it would be very remiss of me not to include something about one of the most successful gundogs ever, the Flat Coated Retriever Irish and English Champion Shargleam Blackcap, bred by Pat Chapman on 26 June 1977 from a mating with Champion Damases Tarquol of Ryshot to Champion Yonday Willow Warbler of Shargleam, the bitch who later was to die so tragically from poison.

Pat Chapman came into Flat Coats in 1974 with the purchase of Yonday Willow Warbler from George Snape and Brett was one of four dogs and eight bitches in the first Shargleam litter which contained Champion Shargleam Black Abby of Withybed, South African Champion Shargleam Black Lace and Challenge Certificate winners Shargleam Black Velvet and Black Orchid.

Brett was actually sold twice as a puppy, the first time to people who would not have been able to give him enough exercise, Pat

Ch Shargleam Blackcap. (Photograph: David Dalton)

discovered, and the second to people who intended kennelling him all day while they were at work, so in the end he stayed at home and Pat showed him. He gained his Junior Warrant at twelve months of age and his first Reserve Challenge Certificate at Crufts in 1979 under Mrs Violet Yates. The first Challenge Certificate was awarded at Southern Kennel Club in the same year by Colin Wells and he was made up at London Kennel Association in the December under Joan Chester-Perks in competition with my Rase Teddy. His qualifier was obtained the previous month.

Crufts 1980 saw Brett take Best of Breed under Mary Grimes, the Group under Margaret Lindsey Smith and Supreme best in Show under Harry Glover. Then after an absence of a year he again won Best of Breed under Joan Mason and the Group under Catherine Sutton in 1982.

Blackcap gained his Irish (Southern) Green Stars in six shows in 1984 where he had one Best of Show, one Reserve Best in Show, three Gundog Groups and two Reserve in Groups. He won his qualifier at an Irish Field Trial to give him his full Irish Title in the December of the same year and a total of 59 Green Stars.

At home he totted up sixty-three Challenge Certificates, fifty Best of Breeds, twenty-two Reserve Challenge Certificates, eighteen Gundog Groups, seven Best in Shows and six Reserve Best in Shows. In addition he won the Pedigree Chum Champion Stakes Final under Joe Braddon in January 1982, the Pro Dogs Final in 1985 under Liz Cartiledge. He was the Breed's leading stud dog in 1982, 1983, 1984, 1985 and 1986, Top Gundog in 1981 and runner-up the following year and held the record for Top Gundog of all time. For all this he was still a pet and slept on Pat's bed until his death in January 1987 at the age of nine.

BIBLIOGRAPHY

Cooke, H. R.   *The Popular Retriever*, 1927
  Notes on Choosing and Breaking a Retriever, 1943
  A few more Short Notes on Retrievers, 1947
Eley, Charles, *History of Retrievers*, 1920
Hutchinsons *Dog Encyclopaedia*, 1934
Johnson, James, *Gundog Breeds. The Illustrated Guide*, 1980
Kennel Club, *Stud Books*, 1874-Present day
Lawe, C. H., *Dog Shows and Doggy People*, 1902
Laughton, Dr Nancy, *Review of the Flat-Coated Retriever*, 1968 & 1980
O'Neill, S.L., *Papers from Flat-Coated Retriever Society Year Books*, 1973, 1974, 1976, 1978
Petch, P., *The Flat Coated Retriever*, 1980
Smith, Sir Henry, *Retrievers and How to Break them*, 1898